Making *Valuing People* Work

Strategies for change in services for people with learning disabilities

Rachel Fyson and Linda Ward

Norah Fry
Research Centre

D1318573

First published in Great Britain in June 2004 by

The Policy Press
University of Bristol
Fourth Floor, Beacon House
Queen's Road
Bristol BS8 1QU
UK

Tel no +44 (0)117 331 4054
Fax no +44 (0)117 331 4093
E-mail tpp-info@bristol.ac.uk
www.policypress.org.uk

© Rachel Fyson and Linda Ward 2004

Cover illustration © Angela Martin

ISBN 1 86134 572 0

Rachel Fyson is a Research Associate and **Linda Ward** is Director, both at the Norah Fry Research Centre, University of Bristol, UK.

This work was undertaken with financial support from the Department of Health. The views expressed are those of the authors and are not necessarily those of the Department of Health.

Cover design by Qube Design Associates, Bristol
Cover illustration: kindly supplied by Angela Martin
Printed in Great Britain by Henry Ling Ltd, Dorchester

Contents

List of tables and good practice checklists · v

Acknowledgements · vi

Executive summary · vii

1 Introduction · 1
Valuing People · 1
About this report · 2

2 Strategic planning in learning disability services · · · · · · · · · · · · · · 5
What is a strategic plan? · 5
Local strategic planning · 6
Joint Investment Plans · 7
Strategic planning and best practice · 15

3 Working together for strategic change: · 19
Learning Disability Partnership Boards
Introduction · 19
Power and decision making · 20
The role of the Chair · 23
Practical arrangements · 26
Representation: people with learning disabilities and family carers · · · · · · 31
Representation: organisations · 34
Missing stakeholders: frontline staff · 36
Accessible information · 37

4 Commissioning and managing for strategic change · · · · · · · · · · · · 41
Introduction · 41
Commissioning and care management · 42
Developing and managing local markets in care · · · · · · · · · · · · · · · · · · 44
Change management · 48
Commissioners' training and professional development needs · · · · · · · · · 51

5 Changing support, enabling choice and independence · · · · · · · · · · 53
Introduction · 53
Person-centred planning · 53
Housing · 59
Day services and employment · 64

6 What happens next?   **71**
    Commissioners and carers look to the future   71
    Beyond 2006   71
    Self-advocates' views on change   73

References   **75**
Appendix A: Further sources of information   **81**
Appendix B: Research methods   **85**

List of tables and good practice checklists

Tables

2.1	Discussion of key principles in Joint Investment Plans (JIPs)	8
2.2	Involvement of stakeholder groups in the development of JIPs	9
2.3	Involvement of people with learning disabilities and families/carers in the development of JIPs	9
2.4	Sub-groups of people with learning disabilities referred to within JIPs	11
2.5	Per cent of JIPs with gaps in information on a range of existing services	12
2.6	Range of per capita expenditure on learning disability services reported in JIPs	12
2.7	Type and extent of problems facing learning disability services as noted by JIPs	14
2.8	Per cent of JIPs with fully costed action plans and identified sources of funding	15
3.1	Backgrounds of Partnership Board Chairs	23
3.2	Practical arrangements for Board meetings	27
3.3	Origin of carers on Partnership Boards	33
3.4	Accessible formats used for Partnership Board materials	37

Good practice checklists

1	Key elements of strategic plans	17
2	Power sharing in Partnership Boards	24
3	Partnership Board Chairs, councillors and senior officers	26
4	Partnership Board meetings and practical arrangements	32
5	Ensuring the representation of people with learning disabilities and carers at Partnership Board meetings	35
6	Accessible information	39
7	Care management and service commissioning	44
8	Managing local care markets	45
9	Contracting 'small print'	48
10	*Valuing People* and change	50

Acknowledgements

Our thanks are due to the many people who contributed to this research and made it possible. In particular, we would like to thank:

- the Department of Health for its financial support of the study as part of its Learning Disability Research Initiative;
- members of our Research Advisory Group for their expert advice and constructive comments throughout the project: Nicola Bailey, Colin Bott, Paul Cambridge, Roger Deacon, Peter Kinsella, Carol Lupton, Elizabeth Lynam, Carol Robinson and Paul Swift; and Steve Strong for informal advice and support;
- Gordon McBride and Brian Myers of Swindon People First for their work on self-advocate involvement in Partnership Boards, and other members of Swindon People First for their participation in a workshop on what 'Change' means, facilitated for us by John Hersov;
- the colleagues who came to the rescue and participated in project fieldwork or analysis in the wake of Ken Simons' sudden death in January 2003: especially Debby Watson for analysis of the Joint Investment Plans; Paul Swift for interviews with commissioners; Beth Tarleton for interviews about the commissioner training programme; Fiona Macaulay for interviews with carers on Partnership Boards; and Rachel Fyson for assuming the lead role and lion's share of the work – way beyond expectations when she joined the project originally;

- all those who contributed specialist knowledge to the expert seminars on day services, employment, housing, quality assurance and person-centred planning;
- the commissioners and Partnership Board Chairs and members who participated in interviews about their views and experiences of the implementation of *Valuing People*;
- course faculty and participants on the National Development Team/Paradigm UK commissioner development programmes;
- Fiona Macaulay for her unfailing secretarial and administrative support to the whole project, including the *Strategies for Change* website; and
- colleagues at the Norah Fry Research Centre, University of Bristol who have shared ideas and offered support throughout.

Our biggest debt, of course, is to the late Ken Simons, our good friend and colleague. It was he who originally conceived the idea behind this project, developed it into a successful funding proposal, and undertook its early stages, until his sudden death in January 2003. If Ken had survived, the project – and this report – would undoubtedly have been very different. Nevertheless, we hope that what we have achieved would have met with his approval, and, more importantly, that it will help others in their efforts to secure better opportunities and services for people with learning disabilities – an endeavour to which Ken was passionately committed.

Executive summary

The White Paper *Valuing People* (DH, 2001b) set out a radical agenda for the development of better support services for people with learning disabilities in England, based on four core principles: rights, independence, choice and inclusion. To address the challenges facing services:

- Local, multi-agency, Learning Disability Partnership Boards were to be set up involving specialist and non-specialist services in both the statutory and voluntary/independent sectors, as well as carers and people with learning disabilities.
- A number of plans and frameworks were to be produced locally outlining the strategies to be adopted on a variety of different issues central to the delivery of better opportunities for people with learning disabilities in the future (for example, employment, housing, person-centred planning).

The Strategies for Change project at the Norah Fry Research Centre, University of Bristol, explored the key issues faced by local Partnership Boards and commissioners in the early days of implementation of the White Paper's provisions to facilitate the strategic changes in services required. It found that:

- *Strategic planning* needs to be based upon accurate information on populations, existing services, unmet need, and costs. Many services lacked the requisite effective information systems, but there were signs of improvement.

- Although *Partnerships Boards* have been established they do not exercise any executive/statutory powers. They can, however, offer a useful forum for debate and provide high-profile recognition of learning disability locally. To increase their effectiveness, they need to define their role more clearly and maximise their influence through effective lobbying of generic public services and scrutiny of local strategic plans. In many areas, sub-groups, working parties or locality groups were more active, and inclusive, than Partnership Boards themselves.
- *People with learning disabilities and carers* were significantly outnumbered by professionals at Partnership Board meetings. There was still work to be done to facilitate their participation on a more equal footing, although progress had been made. Most Boards had made improvements in ensuring that information for meetings was accessible, but more remained to be done here too.
- Independent-sector providers in some areas were developing new services offering real choice and opportunities for genuine social integration. Commissioners need to become more proactive in *managing the market in social care services*, so that innovative, person-centred initiatives become more widespread.
- *Person-centred planning* was being interpreted and implemented in a wide variety of ways. Managers and commissioners need to make clear the distinction between community care

needs assessments and person-centred planning processes. There was a perceived risk that person-centred planning might become watered down or service-led as it is rolled out as an option for people with learning disabilities more widely.

- A lack of capacity in *housing* remained a key issue in many parts of the country. There were, however, indications that commissioners and Partnership Boards were beginning to engage effectively with local authority housing departments and registered social landlords to increase the housing options available for people with learning disabilities locally.

- *Modernising day services* presented a variety of challenges. Family carers were often wary of changes to day service provision that might result in an overall reduction of hours of support available. But in some areas it had proved possible to change the types of activities or support offered *without* reducing the overall hours of service provided.

- Commissioners were well aware of the need to develop more *employment opportunities* for people with learning disabilities in their area. Some local authorities had recognised the impact they could have here in leading the way as local employers themselves. The value of partnership working with generic employment services was also recognised. Local services were clear that they were not in a position to address some of the broader barriers to employment for people with learning disabilities, like the benefits trap; they recognised this as an issue that needs to be addressed by central government nationally.

- People with learning disabilities have often had negative experiences of *change* being foisted on them, without having any say or control over the process. (This has also been true of carers, and sometimes front-line staff.) The pressure to improve services must not overtake the need to listen to people with learning disabilities and ensure that they have as much input as possible into the changes that will affect their lives.

Introduction

Valuing People

In March 2001 the publication of the first White Paper on services for people with learning disabilities in England for 30 years was widely welcomed by people with learning disabilities, family carers, and professionals from within both the statutory and the independent sectors. The agenda for the future development of support services set out in *Valuing People: A new strategy for learning disability for the 21st century* (DH, 2001b) was based on the key principles of rights, independence, choice and inclusion. Few would wish to argue with this value base, or the promotion of person–centred plans as the foundation on which to develop a wide range of alternatives to residential care and traditional day services.

During its creation, *Valuing People* represented a radical departure from the traditional processes of Whitehall policy development. For the first time, people with learning disabilities were actively involved in the working parties from which the White Paper was developed; their views, needs, ambitions, and dreams were reflected in the final document. This desire to shift the locus of power in the direction of service users was also reflected in the simultaneous publication of both accessible CD-ROM and audiotape versions of the White Paper, and an accompanying report *Nothing about us without us* (Service Users Advisory Group, 2001), which clearly outlined the major issues from the perspective of people with learning disabilities themselves.

Subsequent to the White Paper's publication, the involvement of service users has continued to be an important element of the implementation process. At a national level, the Service Users Advisory Group has now been superseded by the National Forum for People with Learning Disabilities. The National Forum provides links between policy makers and a network of regional service user forums, which in turn have links with local self-advocacy groups. It also has its own website which, among other things, provides a national database of self-advocacy groups. People with learning disabilities also sit on the National Learning Disability Task Force, a body which has been set up to oversee the implementation of the White Paper.

Valuing People set out the challenges facing services for people with learning disabilities, which include projected demographic changes and the need to tackle a variety of existing problems: the resettlement of residents still living in long-stay hospitals; the social exclusion experienced by many adults and children with learning disabilities and their families; and the inequitable availability of support services across the country. It also set out the broad directions in which services were expected to travel in order to address these challenges. And it set out a timetable for the production of local strategic plans, each of which was to illuminate the local situation with regard to a particular issue – such as housing and employment – and provide an action plan for implementing proposed changes, improvements or new developments.

However, as the Prime Minister pointed out in his Foreword to *Valuing People*:

> ... the publication of a White Paper, however good its proposals, does not itself solve problems. The challenge for us all is to deliver the vision set out in this document so the lives of many thousands of people with learning disabilities will be brighter and more fulfilling. (DH, 2001b, p 3)

This report is an attempt to examine some of the 'challenges' to which the Prime Minister refers. How can local strategies be developed that reflect the needs, wishes and concerns of local populations? How can people with learning disabilities and family carers be involved in the development of local services? How can the types of support offered to people with learning disabilities be changed, to enable people to take more control over their own lives?

About this report

The *Strategies for Change* research project, the findings from which form the basis of this report, set out to examine these issues of change in learning disability services. In particular, the project focused on the shifts required at a strategic level in order to enable and encourage the changes to

provision and practice required in order to successfully deliver the *Valuing People* vision.

This report concentrates on the following four core themes.

The effectiveness of local strategic planning

Although *Valuing People* provides a national strategic framework for the development of services, it does not describe in detail either the quantity or particular types of services that should be made available, or exactly how local agencies should finance new developments. These kinds of detail are left to local strategic plans. These need, therefore, to be both realistic and robust if they are to produce the changes required. *Chapter 2* examines the learning disability Joint Investment Plans (JIPs) that each local authority was required to produce. The potential for JIPs to act as frameworks for significant change is evaluated, and suggestions made as to the necessary constituents of an effective strategic plan.

The functioning of Learning Disability Partnership Boards

The new Partnership Board structures established by *Valuing People* are responsible for overseeing the creation and implementation of local strategies. They are also intended to act as powerful levers for change, not only by empowering people with learning disabilities and family carers but also by engaging directly with a wide range of generic public services. *Chapter 3* reports on the experiences of self-advocates and carers who sit on local Partnership Boards, and the views of the

one

councillors or senior officers who chair the meetings. Guidance is given on good practice in relation to both practical arrangements for Board meetings and how Boards can exert maximum influence on local policy.

The role of commissioners

A central premise of the research was that one key to the success of *Valuing People* would be the extent to which local commissioners took on board the new vision for learning disability services and implemented the White Paper in a way that would lead to the considerable strategic change undoubtedly needed. *Chapter 4* focuses on the role of commissioners and looks in turn at the relationship between care management and commissioning; managing local markets in care services; change management within existing services; and the training and development needs of commissioners.

Developments in person-centred planning, housing, day services and employment opportunities

The concept of person-centred support for people with learning disabilities lies at the very heart of *Valuing People*. If this idea is not understood and embraced, then the chances of creating services that reflect the true ethos of the White Paper are slim. *Chapter 5* presents evidence of some of the difficulties that have emerged as the theory of person-centred planning is translated into practice, and sets out some of the key arguments and issues around adopting person-centred approaches to support services, focusing in particular on housing

and day services and employment opportunities.

Chapter 6 starts with an overview of various stakeholder views concerning what *Valuing People* has achieved so far, and what issues remain a priority for action. It goes on to suggest how *Valuing People* may be taken forward after 2006 when the Valuing People Support Team, set up to support local implementation of the White Paper, will be dissolved. It concludes with messages from a workshop held with self-advocates about their experiences of change. This highlights the importance of ensuring that service users are empowered to decide what lifestyle changes they want to happen and the need to pace change so that all stakeholders have the necessary time to adjust to new ways of working.

Publications referred to in the text are listed in References. *Appendix A* provides details of a number of websites and organisations providing information that may be of use to those involved in strategic planning within learning disability services. For a full description of the methodologies used in the course of undertaking this research, see *Appendix B*.

Strategic planning in learning disability services

What is a strategic plan?

Valuing People is subtitled 'A new *strategy* for learning disability'. It thus creates an expectation that it will contain, or demonstrate, certain key attributes. Although the term 'strategy' may mean different things to different people – Mintzberg et al (1998) identify no fewer than 10 distinct schools of thought on the topic – a 'strategy' is certainly more than simply a large-scale or long-term plan. In the sense used here, the term 'strategy' implies, or indeed requires, the existence of:

- a guiding vision;
- accurate information regarding the existing situation;
- objective goals;
- clear timetables;
- criteria for measuring progress.

As a national strategic plan, *Valuing People* succeeds very well in providing a coherent and principled guiding vision. The four 'key principles' of rights, independence, choice and inclusion are defined with simple yet eloquent brevity. Collectively, they provide a value base that is reasonable yet inspirational. By choosing to echo O'Brien's 'five accomplishments' (O'Brien, 1987), the 'key principles' provide a link with the past, and so should make the new vision easy for local organisations to

embrace. By adopting a transparently social model of disability and making unambiguous connections to contemporary mainstream political concepts – notably human rights and social exclusion/inclusion – the principles also provide an ideological link between learning disability and generic social issues. This is important. It underlines the fact that people with learning disabilities have the same kinds of needs and aspirations as anyone else. This should make it easier for non-specialist public service providers to understand.

Nonetheless, a comprehensive strategic plan must be more than simply a set of principles, however fine. Given that this was the first White Paper, and indeed the first English *national* strategy, for 30 years, there was in effect no 'old' strategy to be replaced. In terms of objective goals, *Valuing People* had to draw together previously disparate examples of best practice from around the country into a coherent set of desirable, measurable, deliverable outcomes. In this sense, *Valuing People* is perhaps less successful as a strategic tool in that it fails to set numerical targets for, say, housing or other services. It might, for example, have stipulated that, for every x number of people in the general population, y number of supported living placements should be developed. Although such targets may, if taken simply at face value, appear to be the polar opposite of person-centredness, evaluation of the All Wales Strategy (Todd et al, 2000) suggests that the omission of such national numerical targets can limit a strategy's ultimate effectiveness and success on issues of equity.

Since the White Paper has to be implemented not by central government but by local authorities, local health trusts and voluntary and independent sector service providers, it could also reasonably be argued that *Valuing People*, although a national strategy in name, is in fact of greater totemic than practical value. That is to say that its most important role may be in providing:

- a clear political message that the government cares about what happens in the lives of people with learning disabilities; and
- a national, value-based, framework around which more detailed local strategic plans can be developed.

Local strategic planning

At the start of the *Valuing People* implementation programme (in fact, slightly before the delayed publication of the White Paper itself), each English local authority was required to produce a Learning Disability Joint Investment Plan, or 'JIP'. The purpose of this document was to set out a coherent strategy for the future development of local learning disability services, in the light of the guiding vision and key principles described in the White Paper. This was to be

achieved in conjunction with all key stakeholders – including not only the 'usual suspects' from specialist learning disability services in the statutory and voluntary or independent sectors, but also a wide range of generic public services – including housing, education, employment and leisure. Most importantly of all, it was to be produced with the full and active involvement of people with learning disabilities and their families or carers.

Although not explicitly described as 'strategic' plans, JIPs were clearly intended to contain all of the core attributes of a strategy. Guidance issued at the time (Giraud-Saunders and Greig, 2001) emphasised the imperative that JIPs should be written in partnership and reflect local priorities. JIPs were also meant to provide a link with the government's wider agenda of reducing social exclusion, by forming part of the overall framework of Local Strategic Partnerships. These partnerships are part of a programme developed by the Office of the Deputy Prime Minister, intended to strengthen links between statutory and non-statutory agencies in order to better meet the needs of local people and help create sustainable communities (ODPM, 2004). However, the principal role of JIPs was to provide the first stage of an action plan towards the implementation of *Valuing People*. The first JIPs can therefore be regarded in one sense as representing a baseline against which learning disability services could measure future progress.

The first round of JIPs was completed in Spring 2001 and, despite – or perhaps because of – the difficulties that some local authorities experienced in pulling together all the required information, they provided not only a useful snapshot of existing services but also a valuable insight into the strengths and weaknesses of local strategic planning within English learning disability services at that moment in time. The second round of JIPs, which was completed a year later, has not been included in the following analysis, partly because the electronic JIP pro-forma that was used in 2002 meant that less was revealed about individual local authorities' information and planning.

Joint Investment Plans

Our analysis of the JIPs took as its starting point a modified version of the 'core tenets' of strategic planning, as outlined earlier. Our modifications were additions to that basic list of expectations of JIPs as strategic plans – such as the active involvement of people with learning disabilities and their families/carers –that were central to their purpose.

Copies of 104 JIPs were obtained from a potential total of 127, so providing a sample size of 82%. The documents themselves varied enormously in size, content and quality – ranging from glossy, professional publications to a dozen or so sheets of simple type. A standardised tool was developed in order to assist in the analysis, the purpose of which was to enable objective assessment of the extent to which each JIP demonstrated the following elements of a strategic plan:

- a statement of vision or values, designed to underpin local service provision, which was in line with that of *Valuing People*;
- evidence that the JIP had been produced through agreement with key local stakeholders, including people with learning disabilities and carers;
- information about the local population with learning disabilities and its demographic profile in terms of age, ethnicity and support needs;
- documented patterns of current service provision, in particular information regarding people's housing situation and day activities, and of current public expenditure on these services;
- a 'gap analysis' indicating where more or different types of services were required, based on local knowledge of unmet need; and
- a local 'action plan' aimed at tackling the problems identified in the gap analysis, including prioritised tasks, intended outcome measures and practical implementation details (that is, how *much* of *what* was going to be done by *whom* within what *time* scale and using which *resources*).

A guiding vision

Most JIPs opened with a statement about the values/principles that would underpin future developments in local learning disability services. These statements tended to be broadly in line with the key principles set out in *Valuing People*.

two

Table 2.1: Discussion of key principles in Joint Investment Plans (JIPs)

Valuing People's key principles	% of JIPs including a discussion of this principle
Rights	66
Independence	70
Choice	78
Social inclusion	76

None of the JIPs explicitly rejected *Valuing People's* key principles of rights, independence, choice and inclusion, perhaps because the principles were sufficiently broad and well-chosen to be acceptable to all stakeholders. However, as Table 2.1 demonstrates, a significant minority failed to expand upon each principle. Such omissions could generously be interpreted as the result of harried staff working to very tight deadlines. However, such oversight could also suggest that in some cases the principles were 'accepted' but not necessarily fully embraced or embedded in practice. Furthermore, given that only 10% of JIPs brought the four concepts together in a coherent fashion by making specific reference to the adoption of a social model of disability, the explicit adoption of a clear guiding vision or coherent ideology for local strategic plans was far from comprehensively demonstrated.

Stakeholder involvement

Although not an automatic prerequisite of strategic plans, it seemed reasonable to expect that *Joint* Investment Plans would demonstrate the extent and nature of stakeholder involvement, whether as active participants in drawing up the plans, contributors to discussions and consultation events, or signatories to the final document. However, such collective working practices were frequently difficult to discern, not least because only 40% of JIPs gave any clear indication as to who had written – and therefore 'owned' – the document.

It appeared that in many areas the active involvement of stakeholder organisations went little further than cooperation between the twin leviathans of health and social services. This failure to bring on board a wider range of non-specialist services may not be surprising, given the difficulties inherent in achieving effective joint working between pairs of organisations, let alone dozens. However, given that the aim of each JIP was to create a local strategic plan that promoted, among other things, greater social inclusion for people with learning disabilities, the continued (almost exclusive) dominance of specialist services would not appear to offer an auspicious launch pad for the implementation of the White Paper agenda for social inclusion in generic services. Table 2.2 provides details of the extent to which various stakeholder organisations and agencies were involved in the development of local JIPs.

The involvement of people with learning disabilities and their families/carers is a key tenet of *Valuing People* (Table 2.3). Many JIPs provided evidence of their involvement in the development of local plans.

The most common form of involvement was via conferences or workshops held in order to consult with people with learning disabilities. In contrast, only 11% of

Table 2.2: Involvement of stakeholder groups in the development of JIPs

Stakeholder group	% directly involved in JIP development	% indirectly involved or mentioned in passing	% not mentioned as involved in the JIP
Social services	96	1	3
Health authority	89	3	8
NHS trust	68	6	26
Primary care group/trust	58	19	23
Independent sector service providers	34	29	37
Strategic housing authority	25	26	49
Education department (LEA)	16	32	52
Education providers (colleges, and so on)	10	27	63
Learning and skills councils	1	11	88
Careers services (including Connexions pilots)	2	15	83
Employment services	4	20	76
Benefits agency	2	9	89
Economic development agencies	2	7	91
Leisure services	7	20	73
Arts organisations	0	5	95
Advocacy organisations	19	24	57

Table 2.3: Involvement of people with learning disabilities and families/carers in the development of JIPs

Mode of involvement	% involving service users	% involving carers
Conferences, workshops or focus groups to discuss the JIP	56	48
Surveys of service user or carer views and preferences	29	26
Involvement as consultants to JIP process	11	6

service users were involved more directly in the creation of a JIP as consultants to the overall process. A similar pattern emerged with carers, who were slightly less likely than service users to have been involved through any given mechanism. Only one JIP gave any indication that either service users or carers had been paid for their time or otherwise remunerated for their contribution to the process. (The issue of remuneration to carers and service users for their involvement is discussed at greater length in *Chapter 3*.)

The impact of the active involvement of service users and carers in the production of a JIP upon its eventual content is impossible to say, although it is noteworthy that a mere 16% of JIPs were available in formats accessible to service users. (See *Chapter 3* for more on producing accessible information.)

Information on existing populations

In order to facilitate their planning role, JIPs were required to bring together comprehensive data about local people with learning disabilities, existing provision of services and areas of unmet need. Such baseline information is crucial for the development of realistic (and realisable) strategic plans. But in many JIPs this information was incomplete or absent:

- in 45% of JIPs, local data were provided about the prevalence of learning disabilities;
- in 39%, national data were provided about the prevalence of learning disabilities;
- in 43%, evidence was present that some kind of register or database was used as the basis for planning services.

Only 23% of JIPs provided evidence regarding all three of these aspects of populations with learning disabilities.

It was not altogether unexpected that many JIPs were unable to provide such facts. At a national level, no data currently exist that are able to provide an accurate estimate of the number of people with learning disabilities. *Valuing People* suggests that a lower estimate of people with some degree of learning disability would be 25 per 1,000 of the general population, implying a total of at least 1.2 million people with learning disabilities in England. Of these, it is believed that around 120,000 have severe or profound disabilities and need significant help in many or all aspects of daily life, while the remainder have mild to moderate levels of learning disability and are able to live independently with some support.

A major research project has recently been commissioned by the Department of Health designed not only to provide more up-to-date and accurate information about the number of people in England who have learning disabilities, but also to detail people's current use of services, areas of unmet need and life aspirations. (Details of how to find out more about this are provided in *Appendix A*: Survey of People with Learning Difficulties in England.)

The obvious difficulty that many local areas experienced in determining the true size of the population for whom they had to provide support was not unexpected, given the corresponding lack of national data. However, given that JIPs were intended to be key documents in developing coherent strategic plans for future services, the frequent lack of accurate baseline information presented a considerable obstacle to the fulfilment of their purpose. Nearly three quarters of JIPs (73%) gave a figure for the total number of people in the area who were using learning disability services. But the fact that 27% – more than one in four – appeared not to know even this fundamental fact was indicative of the generally poor information systems within local authority social services departments at the time. The population figures quoted in JIPs at times varied considerably from the estimates suggested by national statistics; in some areas the number of people known to learning disability services was as little as half that which might have been expected based on national prevalence rates.

Furthermore, only slightly more than half of JIPs (52%) discussed the likely impact of projected demographic changes (increasing life expectancy, better survival rates for children born with the most profound and complex impairments) upon the population with learning disabilities, and only 41% provided an analysis of the impact of such changes on future demand for services. In view of research evidence indicating both that the incidence of significant learning disabilities is continuing to rise and that carers want more support from statutory services than they are receiving (McGrother et al, 2001), it seems likely that service capacity will become an increasingly important issue for many local authorities.

More detailed data about the needs of different sections of the known local population of people with learning disabilities were patchy at best. Table 2.4 shows the percentage of JIPs that recognised the existence, and particular needs, of various sub-groups within the overall local population with learning disabilities. This information was sometimes numerical, as in: 'There are little number of people with learning disabilities who currently live at home with carers aged 75 or over', but in many cases was simply an acknowledgement that the group of people concerned existed and were in need of services. No JIP provided information about all of the groups identified.

Information on existing services and expenditure

Many JIPs also failed to provide accurate or detailed information about either the extent or the types of local service provision. Again, such information is crucial for the development of strategic plans: without it, it is impossible to assess what needs are already being adequately met or which services might no longer be required and so could enable the redeployment of resources in order to meet future, or currently unmet, needs.

The best JIPs outlined in detail the numbers of people living in different types of accommodation (family home, adult foster placements, supported living, registered care home, nursing home, and so on) and the numbers accessing different types of daytime support services, but these were few and far between. Many others did not even provide global figures for basic services (Table 2.5).

two

Table 2.4: Sub-groups of people with learning disabilities referred to within JIPs

Sub-groups whose specific needs were identified and discussed	% of JIPs
People from minority ethnic communities	52
Young people making the transition from children's services	60
People with profound and multiple impairments	43
People currently living with elderly family carers	28
People with sensory impairments	37
People with mental health needs or challenging behaviour	51
People with mild learning disabilities	21
People with learning disabilities who are parents	11

Table 2.5: Per cent of JIPs with gaps in information on a range of existing services

Type of service	% of JIPs
Housing support (all types)	31
Short break services	72
Support in family home	84
Day centres	45
Employment-related support	49

The availability or otherwise of financial data was equally erratic, with 16% of JIPs providing no figures at all on local patterns of spend by learning disability services. Only 30% of JIPs set out clear and unambiguous details of financial expenditure by both health and social services. Where financial information was given it was frequently incomplete or difficult to decipher. In some cases this was due to a mismatch between local authority and health authority boundaries, or large health authorities being unable to provide disaggregated expenditure figures relating to individual local authority areas.

However, it was clear from those JIPs that did offer some degree of financial detail that spending on services for people with learning disabilities varied significantly from local authority to local authority. Judged against the most recent (2001 Census) figures, expenditure on learning disability services ranged from between £22.49 and £98.35 per capita (of whole population) per annum. Although in some cases the financial data contained in JIPs may not have been wholly accurate (per capita annual expenditure of £138.74, £12.60, £2.65 and £0.08 were assumed to be errata), clear trends were discernible. In general, the highest-spending authorities were to be found in London

and the lowest-spending in the North East, reflecting in large part the different labour costs across regions and echoing the findings of previous research (DH, 1999).

Other variations in levels of expenditure were less readily explicable. They might in part have been due to differences in local populations with learning disabilities resulting from hospital closure, for example, but much of the disparity is likely to reflect actual differences in the quantity and quality of services provided. Table 2.6 shows per capita expenditure in the JIPs for which figures were available (the outliers already mentioned are omitted).

Table 2.6: Range of per capita expenditure on learning disability services reported in JIPs

Per capita expenditure on learning disability services	% of JIPs
£20-29.99	2
£30-39.99	2
£40-49.99	13
£50-59.99	14
£60-69.99	9
£70-79.99	6
£80-89.99	1
£90-99.99	3
Not known	50

On a more general level, a number of 'negative indicators' with regard to patterns of spend and future financing of services were evident: 19% of JIPs expressed concerns about budgetary pressures; 12% made specific reference to budget overspend in the previous or current financial year; 5% spoke of worries about being relatively high-spending authorities; and one indicated that cuts were likely to future learning disability budgets. Arguably, this kind of difficulty was exactly what the JIPs were intended to identify. However, even where financial difficulties were explicitly acknowledged there was no suggestion as to how they might be addressed.

Objective goals, clear timetables and criteria for measuring progress

Taken together, the omission of significant information concerning either current provision of services or current pattern of spend, or both, meant that in many cases the 'gap analysis' and subsequent 'action plan' resembled ill-defined wish lists rather than coherent strategies through which to address identified service deficits.

The JIP gap analyses were supposed to provide a review of the extent and types of local unmet need for services. They were meant to be based on an amalgamation of information from individual assessments, from widespread consultation with people with learning disabilities and family carers, and from provider organisations and other relevant stakeholders. What frequently tended to emerge were lengthy lists of service shortfalls, which did not always clarify the extent or nature of the deficit. For example, a JIP might include commentary to the effect that the area lacked sufficient housing, but fail to say whether what was required was more residential care places, individual tenancies in supported living services, or family-based 'adult fostering' placements.

Despite these limitations, the JIP gap analyses do provide a pertinent overview of the types and extent of difficulties that were facing learning disability services as

the implementation of *Valuing People* got under way.

It is interesting to note the evidence of 'lost opportunity' suggested by this data. For example, 68% of JIPs are shown in Table 2.7 to have noted problems in local housing related to the limited availability of alternatives to residential care. Learning disability services are not in a position to solve this problem alone, yet Table 2.2 showed that in only 25% of cases had strategic housing authorities been directly involved in the development of the JIP, while a staggering 49% of JIPs failed to even mention housing authorities.

Gap analyses were intended to inform the basis of local 'action plans'. These action plans should have constituted the very heart of local strategies for implementing improvements to learning disability services. According to the JIP assessment framework (Giraud-Saunders and Greig, 2001), each action plan should have been fully costed and the source of required funding identified (Table 2.8). This was seldom the case.

In equally scant supply were clear timetables within which action was to occur, and objective criteria against which to measure progress (such as, 'We will provide opportunities for supported employment to *x* more individuals within the next six months' or 'Every carer who wishes to have a carers' assessment will have one within a year').

Table 2.7: Type and extent of problems facing learning disability services as noted by JIPs

Type of problem	% of JIPs identifying
Limited management	
Limited partnership	34
Unresponsive care management	22
Lack of capacity in local service	22
Lack of quality assurance mechanisms	32
Other management limitations	29
Limited choice and control	
General lack of choice	40
Lack of accessible information	70
Lack of person-centred planning	49
Limited support for self-advocacy	49
Limited access to individual advocacy	47
Low take-up of direct payments	58
Other limitations of choice and control	27
Limited residential/housing services	
General shortfall in housing services	35
Limited alternatives to residential care	68
Lack of flexible support for daily living	43
Failure to finish hospital closure programme	11
Other limitations of housing	30
Limited support outside the home	
General shortfall in day services	17
Over-reliance on day centres	42
Social isolation	35
Lack of access to employment	68
Lack of access to social and leisure activities	51
Lack of access to educational opportunities	53
Lack of access to effective transport	42
Other limitations to support outside the home	18
Limited health care	
Problems of access to generic health services	72
Existence of 'health inequalities'	41
Problems of access to mental health services	36
Problems with specialist health care staff	36
Other limitations of health care	33
Limited support to family carers	
Limited access to short break services	61
Lack of information for carers	49
Lack of response to carers' needs	35
Other limitations of support to carers	37
Other issues	57
Limited options at transition	37
Limited support for people from minority ethnic communities	41
Limited support for parents with learning disabilities	19
Lack of attention to bullying/abuse and protection issues	6

Table 2.8: Per cent of JIPs with fully costed action plans and identified sources of funding

Desired area of service improvement	% of JIPs
Housing and support	6
Support for family carers	10
Healthcare	7

Strategic planning and best practice

The overall quality of JIPs varied so widely as to render generalised comments about them virtually meaningless. The best provided a coherent vision for the development of future services, which had clearly taken into account the views of all key stakeholders, including service users and carers as well as a wide variety of service providers. Interviews with commissioners of learning disability services in these local authorities revealed that, even though JIPs ceased to be required by the Department of Health after 2002, JIP action plans continued to be updated regularly and formed the basis of significant service developments:

> "We are sustaining the JIP whether the Department of Health wants it or not. I couldn't chuck it in the bin because it was developed by service users, carers and interested parties." (Commissioner)

A number of commissioners also reported that the JIP process (and the requirement to produce other strategy papers) had highlighted the information deficits that existed in their system:

"In terms of meeting timescales, people were doing bits of work around strategies, but the strategies don't actually say anything, they don't even have information around need, so they're not really implementation strategies." (Commissioner)

In some cases this had led to the creation of a new post of 'Information Officer' and in others had been a catalyst for the development of new computerised systems for recording the outcomes of individual assessments.

It could be argued that the quality or otherwise of learning disability JIPs is now a moot point, given their subsequent demise. However, since then local authorities have still been required to produce a plethora of other strategic plans relating to specific aspects of learning disability service provision, including housing, day services modernisation, workforce planning and quality assurance frameworks. Regional overviews of strategic plans for housing have demonstrated that the quality of strategic plans, like that of the JIPs that preceded them, has continued to vary widely (Harker and King, 2003; Knight, 2003).

Taking into account *all* of the strategy documents which they had written in response to *Valuing People*, many commissioners felt overwhelmed by the sheer volume of such documents that they had been required to produce over a relatively short period of time:

two

"I think the actual creating of the action plans has been problematic you know, we got the person-centred planning strategy off the ground and that one's been OK and we've managed the housing one. I'm still struggling to finish the review of the learning disability team. People are still struggling with quality and workforce, and modernising with day centres is going and people are finding it really difficult to put the time in to actually generate strategies." (Commissioner)

Perhaps more worryingly, many expressed doubts as to whether their plans were likely to be implemented effectively:

"The easy bit was actually sitting down and writing the plans; the hard bit is implementing them and that's going to hit us over the next few years, we just don't have the capacity to deal with it." (Commissioner)

"There's an interesting issue about all these plans, about whether they, I mean, first of all, are they good plans, but also, secondly, do they get implemented?" (Commissioner)

Elsewhere, commentators have argued that the amount of paperwork generated by the rush of strategic plans demanded by *Valuing People* may have displaced direct work with service users (Cumella, 2003). However, despite the pressure on their workloads, some commissioners did acknowledge the benefits of centrally imposed deadlines:

"In some respects you know, the deadlines that they've [DH] given have been useful because the danger is you never actually do anything unless somebody kicks you to do it…. Having said that … I think that it's usually the production of those that's moved us on." (Commissioner)

Whatever the difficulties inherent in their production and implementation, there is little doubt that good-quality strategic plans can be of great help in setting a clear course of action for change. And, whatever changes are being sought, the underlying principles of effective strategic planning remain the same.

Good practice checklist I
Key elements of strategic plans

1. What value base, key principles or guiding vision underpin the strategy?
   - What is the strategy's ultimate goal?
   - Who chose this goal and this value base?
   - Are the goals and value base shared by all those involved in implementing the strategy?

2. Where is the strategy starting from?
   - What services currently exist?
   - What financial resources are currently in use?
   - What human resources are currently in use?

3. What unmet needs for services currently exist?
   - How have these unmet needs been assessed?
   - Which stakeholders have been consulted about this?
   - How might these needs be predicted to change over time?
   - What information systems could help maintain an accurate picture of unmet needs over time?

4. How can these needs be met?
   - What resources (human and financial) will be needed?
   - Can any existing resources be deployed differently?
   - How might further resources be obtained?
     - By using information on unmet need to argue for more funding.
     - By accessing generic services.
     - By developing 'natural supports' in the community.

5. What are the objective goals of the strategy?
   - What end results are desired?
   - How many people will benefit?
   - Which people will benefit?
   - In what ways will they benefit?

6. How can change be delivered?
   - By setting agreed targets, measurable in terms of:
     - Quantity (how many?)
     - Quality (to what standard?)
     - Time (by when?)
   - By identifying a named individual responsible for the delivery of each agreed target.

two

Working together for strategic change: Learning Disability Partnership Boards

Introduction

Valuing People makes plain that people with learning disabilities should be supported to actively participate in *all* decisions that affect their lives, at individual, operational *and* strategic levels:

> People with learning disabilities should be fully involved in the decision-making processes that affect their lives. This applies to decisions on day to day matters such as choice of activities, operational matters such as staff selection and strategic matters such as changes to eligibility criteria. (DH, 2001b, para 4.27)

The White Paper goes much further than previous central government initiatives in recognising both *service users* and *family carers* as key stakeholders within learning disability services who should be actively involved in decision making and planning. But if *Valuing People*'s core principles of rights, independence, choice and inclusion are to become a reality for people with learning disabilities, a wide range of *non-specialist* public services need to actively adopt this agenda too.

To create a sustainable arrangement for the involvement of all the various stakeholder groups in local strategic planning for learning disability services, Learning Disability Partnership Boards were to be established in every local council with responsibility for social services by October 2001(HSC 2001/016: LAC [2001]23). These were a new inter-agency structure, whose membership was to include not only the 'usual suspects' from specialist learning disability services in the statutory and non-statutory sector but also representatives from a wide range of mainstream services that people with learning disabilities should be able to access, including housing, education, leisure and employment. Furthermore, all Partnership Boards were required to include among their membership at least two people with learning disabilities and at least two carers. The guidance issued for the selection of people with learning disabilities and carers to sit on Partnership Boards was as follows:

> Both groups are to be full members of the Board and may take on particular roles. Boards are expected to ensure that the appropriate mechanisms and

support are made available so that both groups play a full part in all discussions and decisions and adequately reflect the views of other local people with learning disabilities and carers. (HSC 2001/ 016: LAC [2001]23, p 5)

The establishment of Partnership Boards was mandatory, as was the involvement of people with learning disabilities and carers within them.

However, most of the operational details relating to the scope and format of meetings were left to the discretion of local authorities. In order to assist in what for some was a new way of working, guidance was issued on partnership working with people with learning disabilities (Aitchison, 2001). Information on supporting and working with carers (Ward, 2001) and people from Black and minority ethnic communities (Mir et al, 2001) had already been published alongside the White Paper itself. The *Valuing People* Support Team also issued advice on the working of Partnership Boards, which included the following statement:

> It is particularly important to try and ensure that the voices are heard of people with more complex needs (including people who do not use verbal communication) and those whose behaviour represents a challenge to services. (DH, 2002a)

This was not a decree that those with the most profound degrees of disability should necessarily be Board members, but a

reminder that their needs and wishes should not be overlooked.

This chapter explores the working of Partnership Boards from the perspectives of self-advocates, carers, commissioners of learning disability services and Board Chairs on broad cross-cutting themes. Each section concludes with suggestions for good practice or a list of issues that may be useful for those involved in Partnership Boards to consider. (For details of materials produced nationally to aid critical reviews of Partnership Board operational practice, see *Valuing People* Support Team, 2003.)

Power and decision making

Learning Disability Partnership Boards are not statutory bodies. They do not have the legal powers necessary to make binding decisions about the use of public monies or to require other agencies or organisations to act at their behest. Partnership Boards may discuss any issue pertinent to learning disabilities and are responsible for overseeing the development of local strategies and action plans. But if these plans require a commitment of local authority resources, they cannot be put into operation without the approval of relevant council executives or committees. The potential influence of Partnership Boards, therefore, lies in their ability to bring together a wide range of stakeholders, in a spirit of cooperation, to develop innovative and empowering approaches to meeting the individual support needs of all people with learning disabilities, rather than in any exercise of direct power. Unlike other partnership initiatives, such as those developed for mental health services, the work of Learning Disability Partnership Boards is not reinforced by National Service Framework status. This was widely regarded by commissioners and Chairs as unfortunate, particularly because of the message it sent to health services, namely, that learning disability services did not have to be among their key priorities.

Many people involved in Partnership Boards appeared unhappy that their function was largely one of guidance and scrutiny rather than active management and decision making. Commissioners and Chairs alike lamented this lack of power:

> "I'd have liked to have seen Partnership Boards as statutory decision-making bodies, so having some delegated powers from county councils and health." (Commissioner)

> "It could not make a budgetary commitment which would affect the County Council's budget, nor could it with the PCT [primary care trust] either." (Chair)

Some carers felt that they had been misled about the nature of the Partnership Board's role:

> "It said in the White Paper that the Partnership Boards are meant to be decision-making bodies, but they have given them no power." (Carer)

And, for others, the lack of power, decision-making capacity and

transparency about where decisions *were* taken was a cause of frustration:

> "I am becoming a bit disillusioned in the fact that I think that there seems to be a lot of talk and no action and that has always been the case with things that I have been involved in as a carer." (Carer)

> "I think there is an executive committee that operates. This has been one of my questions, what does it do? We never see any minutes out of it, but it consists of the top people in the council.... I think the issues are taken to there, they are decided there and then they are sent to the Partnership Board for them to give the OK. But it is not clear exactly what does happen." (Carer)

The only evidence of clear decisions being taken by Partnership Boards was in relation to how Learning Disability Development Fund (LDDF) monies should be spent locally. LDDF was new money for learning disability services (up to £50 million per annum), announced in the White Paper, specifically for the purposes of promoting service change. *Valuing People* stipulates that priorities for the use of such monies include modernising day services, re-provision of long-stay hospital places, developing supported living, promoting self-advocacy, introducing person-centred planning and enhancing leadership within learning disability services.

> "They had a list a couple of meetings ago of projects that were

favoured by the officers and we were all able to vote on them for the next financial year, which is really a powerful way of democratically choosing exactly where the money goes." (Carer)

However, there was generally little evidence that direct decisions were made in relation to other financial or service issues:

"There hasn't been any sign of any really momentous or hard decisions being made at the Partnership Board." (Carer)

What tended to take the place of decisions at Partnership Board meetings were more generalised *discussions* about the issues facing learning disability services. Self-advocates interviewed in the study did not express any particular concerns about this but other self-advocates (for example, Aspis, 2002) have pointed out that being able to *participate* in meetings is not sufficient: true partnership requires that self-advocates are empowered to both understand the system and have an opportunity for their views to contribute to change.

"I think people are trying, but people [other members of the Board] do seem to have their own agendas, which makes it hard." (Self-advocate)

Other Board members were critical of the 'talking shop' nature of many meetings. One carer described how the Partnership Board had spent so long building harmonious relations between participants

that disagreement began to feel like a transgression. And a number of interviewees expressed the belief that meetings were more about being seen than about action or decisions:

"Learning Disability Partnership Board; it's very nice to see people, but really it's two hours of just sharing information." (Commissioner)

It was perhaps inevitable that early Partnership Board agendas would be dominated by the demands by central government that Partnership Boards scrutinise and approve key local strategies, including those for housing, modernisation of day services, quality assurance and workforce planning.

This phenomenon has been noted elsewhere (see, for example, Learning Disability Task Force, 2003). However, it is important that, as time goes on, this does not become an established way of working and that issues important to people with learning disabilities are given a place on the agenda:

"I have a feeling that probably service users aren't fully aware of how to go about getting things onto the agenda, in advance." (Carer)

"If I'm being cruel, the agenda group is everybody other than the users themselves." (Commissioner)

There were some examples of good practice, however. One Partnership Board limited the agenda to three items, one of which was nominated by people with learning disabilities so as to enable them to participate actively. In another area the self-advocacy group reported that a learning disability service manager met with the group before each meeting and talked through the agenda in order to ensure their views were prominent during Board meetings. This ensured that self-advocates had a chance to ask for clarification on any issues about which they were unsure.

There was also limited evidence that some Partnership Boards were successfully exercising a degree of power through effective scrutiny of local issue-specific strategies:

> "Education came up with a plan; they came and did a presentation for the Partnership Board and we virtually threw it out because it was just surface work. It was the kind of stuff that you could download off the Internet and just read it out word for word. That is all they had got.... So we said that they would have to go away and do it again." (Carer)

Partnerships Boards, in crude legal terms, do not wield a great deal of power. However, the very fact that members of so many organisations participate in meetings means that Boards can be highly *influential*. Because the 'power' of Boards is not immediately obvious, it is important that the way in which the Board *can* influence services is explained as clearly as possible to people with learning disabilities and family carers. Only if all Board members are equally aware of how its 'power' operates

can they all hope to have equal influence in determining how those 'powers' are put into effect.

The role of the Chair

Government directives indicated that Partnership Boards should be chaired by 'a senior local government officer or elected member' (HSC 2001/016: LAC [2001]23, p 3). This guidance on selecting Chairs sent out two clear messages: first, that learning disability services are part of a local authority's social care remit rather than primarily a health responsibility, as was the case in the past; second, that learning disability issues are sufficiently important to warrant the attention of senior local government figures.

The Chairs who were interviewed as part of this research project had come to the role with the following backgrounds:

Table 3.1: Backgrounds of Partnership Board Chairs

Who chairs the Partnership Board?	Number
Elected councillor	7
Council Chief Executive	1
Director of Social Services	2
Assistant Director of Social Services	6
Head of Disability Services	1
Commissioner of Learning Disability Services	1
Total	**18**

Note: Chairs in two areas were not available for interview.

The councillor Chairs were drawn from across the political spectrum. In some areas it had been decided that a councillor from the ruling party, often the person who held the social services portfolio in

Good practice checklist 2
Power sharing in Partnership Boards

Power: explain to all Partnership Board members
- What powers the Partnership Board has.
- What powers the Partnership Board does *not* have.
- What binding decisions can be made by the Partnership Board.
- What decisions will need to be ratified elsewhere.
- The *reasons* why certain decisions are made in other places (that is, the need for political and financial scrutiny by elected members of the local council).
  Remember: This information will need to be made available in easily understood and accessible formats (Rodgers et al, 2004).

Voting
- If the Partnership Board makes decisions, who has a vote?
- Should different people be allowed to vote on different issues? (For example, people with learning disabilities and carers get to vote on all issues; professionals get to vote only on issues that directly affect their department or organisation; the Chair has only a casting vote.)

The agenda
- Who sets the agenda for Board meetings?
- What time is made available for local issues rather than those determined by the central government schedule for implementing *Valuing People*?
- What systems exist to enable people with learning disabilities and carers to get items on to the agenda?
- Are such systems transparent?
- Could the existing agenda system be made simpler?
  Do the views of people with learning disabilities and carers *really* count when decisions are made? If not what could be done to make this happen?

cabinet or who chaired the social services sub-committee, should always chair the Partnership Board; in others, the role had been open to volunteers. In a few areas, Councillors from all parties attended Board meetings, a situation which allowed for a smooth transition between Chairs when council elections resulted in a change of party in power locally.

Some councillors already had a strong grasp of learning disability issues before taking on the task of chairing the Partnership Board; for others is was a whole new world:

> "One of the things we're having to learn is that we're dealing with Councillors who know, who think they know something about community care. In reality what

they know is the, you know, *The Sun* or *The Mirror* headlines." (Commissioner)

"It is a very heavy responsibility as I saw it and a lot of hours were put in, especially speaking to and working with people with learning disabilities, the representatives and the carers." (Chair)

What appeared to matter most, however, was not previous experience but willingness to devote time and energy to promoting and pursuing *Valuing People*'s core principles and goals. Although some Chairs had no prior knowledge of learning disability issues, at the time our interviews took place, all were well-versed in the White Paper's priorities and how these related to their local situation.

Most Chairs who were local government officers had acquired their role as a function of their wider job description:

"I suppose ... the guidance seems to suggest, it was fairly explicit, there was a senior manager from a local authority who would have to be the Chair and so – as Assistant Director with responsibility for learning disabilities – it was agreed that I would chair it." (Chair)

It is debatable, however, whether a Head of Disability Services or a Commissioner for Learning Disability Services can be regarded as sufficiently senior to be able to effectively wield the type of influence demanded by the role. Whatever the abilities of the individuals concerned, a more senior person is likely to have

stronger links and greater influence beyond the narrow confines of specialist learning disability services. This also avoids other difficulties of the kind noted by one commissioner Chair:

"I've agreed to take on the role of chairing the Partnership Board but I'm not sure that I should be chairing because I think there could be conflicts between commissioning and chairing." (Commissioner Chair)

Valuing People's chances of creating sustainable changes in the lives of people with learning disabilities rests in large part upon the ability to get issues that have traditionally been regarded as relevant only within a separate (some would say Cinderella) service adopted as part of the mainstream. The example of a Partnership Board being chaired by the local authority Chief Executive is exceptional (just one in our sample), but if such a lead were followed by more local authorities it would certainly send a clear signal that learning disability issues are high on the public sector agenda.

The personal attributes of any Chair are undoubtedly important, as more than one person noted:

"Some Chairs of Partnership Boards just see their role as being to facilitate the meetings, perhaps help write the minutes or something like that, whereas others seem to take a much more active role in the implementation of stuff which comes out of the Boards." (Chair)

three

The appointment of the right Chair can be vital in determining the effectiveness of a Board's work and the extent of its influence. Having a Chair who is willing and able to put in the necessary time to promote the learning disability agenda in other forums can confer significant advantage. Indeed, the access that *senior* local government officials have to their peers elsewhere in the upper echelons of the local authority is what enables them to be of such great potential benefit to their Board.

A significant number (although still less than half) of Partnership Boards which were involved in this research had also appointed a learning disabled Co-Chair.

Such an arrangement sends a clear and unambiguous message that people with learning disabilities are central to all aspects of Board work. It may also be important in encouraging other people with learning disabilities to have the confidence to speak up at meetings and in demonstrating the capabilities of people with learning disabilities to any sceptics from generic services.

Practical arrangements

Many issues concerning the satisfactory organisation and conduct of Partnership Board meetings may seem little more than common sense, but the extent to which

Good practice checklist 3
Partnership Board Chairs, councillors and senior officers

Choosing a Chair
- Who decides whether the Chair should be an elected member or a senior official?
- Who decided that the present incumbent should chair the Partnership Board?
- Is there any mechanism whereby the Board can select a new Chair should it wish to do so?
- Does someone with a learning disability co-chair the Partnership Board? If not, why not?

Questions to consider about councillors
- Is this a political appointment?
- If so, what arrangements are there to ensure a smooth hand-over if there is a change in political control of the council?
- Have councillors of all major political parties been encouraged or invited to attend Partnership Board meetings?
- What background does the councillor have in learning disability issues? (He or she may need an induction, including visiting local services, meeting people with all degrees of learning disability, and meeting carers.)

Questions to consider of senior officers
- Is this the most senior person available? How will this person promote the learning disability agenda beyond the confines of social services?

basic requirements (of accessibility, for example) were not being met was quite astonishing. Although Chairs almost unanimously expressed pride in how they had developed inclusive practices for Board meetings, this positive spin often did not match up to accounts given by the self-advocates interviewed.

Self-advocates frequently reported significant difficulties with the practical arrangements for Partnership Board meetings (Table 3.2). Examples emerged of doors too narrow to allow wheelchairs through; stairs without lifts or ramps available; and, most commonly, poor acoustics. Several self-advocates reported the disempowerment of being unable to hear other people or make themselves heard in large spaces where many people were gathered:

> "They speak so quietly in these meetings, because they are all so far away. We should be closer, like we are now, so I can hear better. But half the time I can't hear it." (Self-advocate)

Under the government's directive, Partnership Boards were required to meet at least four times each year but, beyond this, practical arrangements could largely be organised around the needs and wishes of local stakeholders, with the suggestion that 'non-traditional' ways of working should be considered. This resulted in considerable variations between Boards' *modi operandi*.

Frequency and duration of meetings

Although Partnership Boards were *required* to meet only quarterly, many had decided to meet at more frequent intervals so that they could respond more rapidly to local issues.

> "My biggest argument is that the Partnership Board only meets once every three months, which is not nearly enough.... There doesn't seem time for discussion." (Carer)

More frequent meetings also meant that agendas and the duration of meetings could be kept shorter, so that Board members with a learning disability would be less likely to find the meetings too long to cope with.

Getting the length of meetings right meant confronting competing and contradictory pressures:

> "I think the struggle is the agenda; the agenda is massive. I get

Table 3.2: Practical arrangements for Board meetings

Arrangements	Variations
Frequency of meetings	Monthly to quarterly
Duration of meetings	2 hours to all day
Number of people with learning disabilities	1-6 (usually 2)
Number of carers	2-5 (usually 2)
Total number at meetings	15-40+
Meeting venue	Fixed or varied

criticised for not consulting people and then the next day I get criticised for over-consulting people and people haven't got time to come on board and do things." (Commissioner)

What seemed to work well in many cases was the use of sub-groups to enhance the participation of people with learning disabilities and carers:

"What the Partnership Board supporters are doing now is splitting us up into different sub-groups and I think everybody here was in a sub-group actually.... That meeting was easier to understand and easier to take part in." (Self-advocate)

However, such a system almost inevitably resulted in a longer meeting than one conducted within more traditional formats:

"They tend to be all-day affairs, well 10.00am–3.00pm. They are quite long, but that was the choice of the Board members, because we felt that that way there was also a chance to chat informally over lunch break and also we could build in breaks during the course of the day, and I think that is just to cover all the business we need to get through." (Carer)

At the same time, very frequent or very long meetings might reduce the chances of getting senior figures from non-specialist services to attend:

"It's a very powerful forum, but the difficulty is trying to get people round the table. And I don't think that's a commitment problem, I think that's a time problem." (Commissioner)

While it is completely reasonable to expect representatives from housing, education, leisure, and so on, to be present at Partnership Board meetings, there is undoubtedly a limit to their capacity. To look at this from another angle: how many senior managers within learning disability services would be willing and able to spend half a day *every* month attending, say, a leisure services committee at which learning disability issues were not always even mentioned?

In response to these difficulties, most areas had developed systems of sub-committees or locality groups. Sub-committees were convened on either a temporary or a permanent basis to examine particular issues in greater depth, produce reports or plans, and refer their ideas to the main Board meeting for ratification:

"I am on a couple of the sub-groups and one of them is excellent – the good health sub-group. Anything that I put forward is really well thrashed out there and then, but this is a nice small group, you know there are only eight of us and that is obviously much easier to handle than 30-odd people there." (Carer)

Locality groups, which were more common in rural areas with scattered populations, brought people together on the basis of geography to discuss issues that were topical or relevant within that particular district:

> "We've made it clear that part of the role of the locality groups is, they can act as pressure groups in their own right so we've invited district councillors, for example." (Chair)

Both systems appeared to have the potential to work equally well, depending – as ever – on the commitment and enthusiasm of those involved.

Timing and location of meetings

The timing and location of meetings could also be occasions for a certain degree of friction. Clearly, when a large number of people need to gather together, the timing and/or venue is always likely to be inconvenient for someone. However, it was clear that certain factors were likely to consistently disadvantage certain groups. For example, although an out-of-town venue might offer easier parking for professionals attending Board meetings, the lack of public transport might place people with learning disabilities, and some carers, at a considerable disadvantage. Similarly, although meetings in the middle part of the day – from 11am to 2pm, say, with a half-hour lunch break – often suited full-time carers whose sons or daughters attended traditional day centres, such timings were highly inconvenient for carers, or people with learning disabilities, who worked. This may be one reason for the predominance on Partnership Boards of older carers, who were no longer in

paid employment. But, as ever, pressures could operate in opposite directions:

> "The timing of the meeting is generally made so that it is actually where the majority, carers and people with learning disabilities, have got better access to the timings, purely and simply because if it was not in the daytime people couldn't make it, because caring issues become more difficult." (Carer)

> "We did lose an excellent carer because she works full-time and the meetings are always held during the day." (Carer)

Money matters

Both self-advocates and carers were often seriously disadvantaged in comparison with professionals who attended Partnership Board meetings by the lack of adequate financial support systems for their attendance. The costs of effective involvement have been highlighted by self-advocacy groups (see, for example, People First, Scotland, 2003), yet it was frequently clear that insufficient attention had been given to the financial implications of involving people with learning disabilities and carers in meetings.

Financial recognition, whether in terms of payment to Board members or of meeting their participation costs, is important. Overlooking money matters may preclude the involvement of some people; attention to money demonstrates an acknowledgement of the value of the

three

contribution of the person being reimbursed or paid.

Four main issues emerged in relation to the financial arrangements for self-advocates and carers who attended Partnership Boards.

Costs of support workers

Only a minority of self-advocacy groups in the areas visited reported that they were given specific financial help to provide support workers for group members attending Partnership Board meetings. Where this did not happen, disagreements arose at times as a result of the competing demands of self-advocacy groups' own priorities and the local authority's preference that they become actively involved in their partnership processes. Many self-advocacy groups are small, have few financial resources, and have much work to do over and above their involvement in Partnership Boards. If they are to consult with the wider population with learning disabilities and represent them effectively at Partnership Board meetings, then a service-level agreement on support for participation is probably desirable.

Expenses

Both self-advocates and carers often reported problems in recovering expenses incurred as a result of their Board work:

> "Everyone else here has an office provided, they all have paper, they have sundries provided, they have a system for expenses of any kind, I said we haven't and this is not right.

They all said yes, we all absolutely agree, we need to set something up, I did a template, nothing has happened! I would imagine that most Boards are the same. It is not for lack of good will, they all agreed, they were 100% but it is getting someone to do it." (Carer)

In (more than) one case the reimbursement of travel expenses took more than 18 months, causing considerable hardship for individual carers and putting strain on the fragile finances of the self-advocacy groups concerned.

Payment for attending meetings

Paying both carers and people with learning disabilities to attend Partnership Board meetings is good practice, but was unusual. In the course of this research only one Board was identified that followed best practice in this area:

> "The argument was that, if we are here as equal members, everybody else is here on a paid basis, the carer is the expert, and so the carer should be paid. We negotiated a payment.... And they have also agreed with the learning disability partnership funding; part of it – I think £10,000 – has been set aside to pay the user representatives on the Board." (Carer)

Many Chairs and commissioners believed that trying to pay people who, in many cases, were recipients of means-tested benefits was too complicated an undertaking. But clearly, if some areas could overcome existing obstacles to making such payments, others could do so too. (For advice on how to make such payments without disrupting benefits, see Scott, 2003.)

Loss of earnings

Although affecting only a minority of carers or people with learning disabilities, potential loss of earnings is one of many factors that could preclude the involvement of some individuals.

> "I think they are paid travel expenses, but they aren't compensated for any loss of earnings. That is the fundamental thing." (Chair)

If *Valuing People*'s aims of increasing social inclusion through employment are to be realised, this may affect increasing numbers of people with learning disabilities in years to come. One way of addressing this issue is to encourage employers (particularly in the public sector) to allow a certain amount of paid time off work for people to attend Partnership Board meetings. This had been successfully adopted as best practice in one council area, and is in line with concessions made for other types of recognised public service, for example, trade union activities or being a councillor or a magistrate.

Representation: people with learning disabilities and family carers

Professionals dominate almost all Partnership Boards, at least in numerical terms. The smallest number of individuals at Partnership Boards reported by interviewees was 15 plus, but numbers were more often 20–30 and in several cases reached over 40. Since the numbers of service users, self-advocates and carers present at meetings tend to be limited, it is important that those who do attend are able to effectively represent the views of the wider groups of which they are a part.

Self-advocates

Self-advocacy group members were often the only people with learning disabilities at Partnership Board meetings. This had the potential to create difficulties when self-advocates were no longer themselves service users and had no easy way of ascertaining the views of other people with learning disabilities who continued to receive services locally. The issue of representation was less acute in areas where well-supported and properly funded initiatives were in place to enable self-advocates to consult with the wider population of people with learning disabilities; but such examples were rare. One local authority had successfully pioneered a service users' parliament, whose democratically elected members met prior to Partnership Board meetings and decided what views they wished Board members to represent. However, it was more common for self-advocacy organisations to struggle to find the time and money needed to support effective individual attendance at meetings, let alone consult or report back information more widely.

This can be an important issue because self-advocates, as individuals, are not necessarily representative of the wider

Good practice checklist 4
Partnership Board meetings and practical arrangements

Practical issues

- Is the building fully wheelchair accessible?
- How good are the acoustics in the meeting room?
- Is there an induction loop for people who have hearing difficulties?
- Are microphones available for people who are not used to speaking up in public and may find it difficult to project their voice?
- Is the room big enough to split the meeting into smaller groups if this is desired?
- How good are the public transport links?
- Is car parking available?

Timing, frequency and duration of meetings

- For which groups are current meetings most/least convenient?
- Which groups are excluded completely by the current timing of meetings?
- Have alternative times or venues been considered?
- Would key stakeholders attend more regularly if meetings were shorter or less frequent?
- Would some issues be better dealt with in sub-groups or locality meetings, which involve more people who are actively interested in a particular topic?
- What would be the implications of limiting the number of items on the agenda?

Financial issues

- Can Board members claim travel expenses?
- Can Board members claim other out-of-pocket expenses such as printing out minutes and papers sent by e-mail?
- How long does it take for travel and other costs to be reimbursed?
- Are Board members paid a fee for attending meetings?
- Can Board members claim for loss of earnings incurred through attending meetings?
- Are Board members who work for the local authority entitled to paid time off work to attend meetings?
- Who pays for the cost of support workers for Board members with a learning disability?
- Are carers given access to a 'sitting service' to enable them to attend meetings?
  Both Partnership Board membership and individual circumstances change over time. Are all practical issues regularly reviewed? If not, they should be.

population of people with learning disabilities in their area. The majority of those interviewed for this research were relatively young, white, males with good verbal skills; most were not physically disabled. Women with learning disabilities, people from Black and minority ethnic communities, or people with communication difficulties participated in the research only as part of larger groups, never when only one or two individuals met the research team. No older people with learning disabilities participated at any point.

There is no reason to believe that the self-advocates involved in this research were an atypical sample. Issues of age, gender, race and impairment exist both within the self-advocacy movement and within learning disability services as a whole. More undoubtedly needs to be done to ensure that Partnership Boards do not simply reflect the white male hegemony of so many other social and political structures (*Valuing People* Support Team, 2004). As Mir et al (2001) point out, extra efforts may need to be made to encourage and enable the involvement of people from Black and minority ethnic communities: the same could also be said of the need to engage with women, older people and people with more severe or profound learning disabilities.

Given that people with more severe or profound learning disabilities are less likely to be Board members themselves, it is important that their needs are adequately represented by other means. There is an increasing body of work that demonstrates how people with more severe impairments can be supported to communicate their wishes and choices (for example, Bradshaw, 2001; Cameron and Murphy, 2002). Once elicited, these choices need to be communicated to Partnership Boards in order to ensure that the needs and wishes of this section of the local learning disability population do not continue to be overlooked.

Carers

Carer members of Partnership Boards were not always representatives of other carers or carer groups in the local community either. Of those interviewed for the research, almost half had simply been invited to become members of their local Partnership Board rather than being nominated by a carers group, for example (see Table 3.3), most often because of previous involvement with local statutory services:

> "[It was] sort of suggested that I might like to go on it and I didn't know much about it. But I did allow my name to go forward ... and I found myself on the board, rather surprisingly." (Carer)

Fewer than half of the carers interviewed (seven out of 17) were part of any formal network or group of carers. This meant that, for the majority, it was simply not possible to fulfil a representative function:

Table 3.3: Origin of carers on Partnership Boards

How carers came to be on Partnership Boards	Number
Invited on to Board by social services	8
Nominated by established carer group	6
Elected by ballot of all carers	0
Elections proposed, but no other candidates came forward	2
Unclear/did not say	1
Total	**17**

"I don't feel like I represent a group of carers and I have always made that really clear, that I don't feel that I should represent other carers. I am a carer member of the Board." (Carer)

Indeed, one carer had been told by the Partnership Board that a representative function was beyond their remit:

"When the Partnership Board started I was the only carer there and it was said that you're not representing people as such, it's more or less if you think it's good for carers that's it." (Carer)

Most carers who were not part of any wider group remained uncomfortably aware of this democratic deficit:

"This is one of the problems that I have been raising right from joining; that the only thing I can say is: 'This is my view, not the people's view'." (Carer)

As was the case with self-advocates, the characteristics of carers who sat on Partnership Boards did not necessarily reflect the diversity of the wider carer community. However, in some places steps had been taken to achieve better representation:

"We have now co-opted another member of an ethnic minority because [name of local area] as you know, is nearly 50% ethnic minority in population, so another parent has joined. And we have got some younger parents." (Carer)

Perhaps more importantly, the carers *did* have very diverse caring experiences: caring for offspring with profound and multiple impairments, Down's syndrome, early onset dementia, autistic spectrum disorders; parents of school leavers enrolled at local colleges of further education; and, in one or two cases, parents whose adult children had successfully moved away from the family home into supported living arrangements.

Representation: organisations

The fact that people with learning disabilities and carers sit alongside generic providers of housing, education, leisure and other public services has the potential to impact considerably upon the awareness such services have of the needs of people with learning disabilities within the local community. However, not everyone believed that attendance at Partnership Board meetings would translate into a more generalised positive attitude towards learning disability within generic services:

"The people that need to be represented are there, both at the Partnership Board and at sub-group level, but that doesn't necessarily mean that it begins to be a key priority for any of the organisations that they're representing." (Chair)

That said, strategies developed in such a mixed forum would appear likely to have a greater chance of promoting independence and social inclusion than those developed solely within the confines of specialist learning disability services. In particular, several authorities reported successful

---

Good practice checklist 5

Ensuring the representation of people with learning disabilities and carers at Partnership Board meetings

Representation of people with learning disabilities and carers at Partnership Board meetings

- How do Board members with a learning disability represent the local population of self-advocates, service users and other people with learning disabilities?
- How do carer members represent the local population of carers?
- What mechanisms exist to enable people with learning disabilities and carers to both consult with and report back to the populations they represent?
- Are self-advocacy, service user and carer groups supported financially by statutory services? If not, why not?
- How are the views, needs and wishes of people with more severe or profound learning disabilities represented?
- How are the views, needs and wishes of older carers and older people with learning disabilities represented?
- How are the views, needs and wishes of people from Black and minority ethnic communities represented?
- How are the views, needs and wishes of women with learning disabilities represented?

engagement with either district council housing departments or local housing associations (see *Chapter 5* for more on housing).

As with the production of JIPs, some areas had had greater success than others in involving a wide variety of organisations in Partnership Boards. In a number of local authorities engagement was the norm across all statutory services:

> "You think of a department and nine times out of ten they are there." (Carer)

Although many Partnership Boards reported non-attendance by various representatives of non-specialist local authority departments or statutory and non-statutory organisations, no pattern of

consistent non-attendance emerged. Where there were difficulties with engaging particular organisations, these often appeared to relate to long-standing local problems between social services and the department or organisation concerned:

> "There is not a good relationship between social services and education, for various reasons." (Carer)

In such cases, only local solutions are likely to lead to the development of effective partnership working, although books such as *Partnership made painless* (Harrison et al, 2003) can offer useful starting points for action.

Missing stakeholders: frontline staff

The quality of support experienced by people with learning disabilities depends in large part upon the qualities of frontline support staff. And frontline staff, arguably, have most to fear from moves to empower people with learning disabilities. It is they who must change their culture and working practices and perhaps agree changes to their terms and conditions of employment or hours of work.

Despite this, no Partnership Boards included representatives from frontline care staff, although in one area frontline staff were involved in locality groups. This one example aside, no Chairs or commissioners raised the issue of the lack of involvement of frontline staff as an oversight or shortcoming within their system. The issue was, however, raised by more than one carer:

> "Somewhere I think there should be some representative from the staff side of things. Other than management there doesn't seem what I call lower-down people, the people that are our usual first point of contact; there doesn't seem to be anybody from that particular section." (Carer)

The lack of proactive involvement of frontline staff in strategic planning was matched by an impression in a small number of localities that these staff were regarded as barriers to effective change. Indeed, in more than one area, where commissioners felt that they had been unable to secure the desired culture shift within their existing workforce, steps had been taken to terminate contracts when services were restructured:

> "When we did the hospital re-provision programme we didn't include ... a ... transfer of staff who are employed by the hospital to the housing association. Quite deliberately, we saw it as more cost-effective to pay them off, primarily because we didn't believe that we could change the culture and many of them were more institutionalised than the service users." (Commissioner)

This is clearly not a desirable strategy, particularly in areas which are already experiencing problems in recruiting and retaining sufficient numbers of qualified staff; and it is to be hoped that most services will find less draconian ways of implementing change. However, such drastic measures do serve to highlight the importance of bringing frontline staff on board when radical changes to patterns of services and support are being proposed.

It would seem desirable to include frontline staff in strategic planning bodies, precisely because they are the workers who will be most directly affected by any new service developments, and because they may be best placed to know how to inculcate cultural change. Clearly, frontline staff alone should not determine the direction of service developments, but neither should their views be overlooked completely, as sometimes seemed to be the case. If Partnership Boards are aiming to change working practices and cultures, it is worth considering how they can proactively involve frontline staff in the process.

One option adopted in some areas was to open Partnership Board meetings to the public, so that any people with learning disabilities, carers or frontline staff who wished to do so could attend as observers. If meeting times are widely advertised in advance, this provides a relatively easy way of engaging with larger numbers of people. However, some self-advocates expressed a dislike of public meetings; they felt it caused the balance of power to shift away from people with learning disabilities and towards carers, who attended in greater numbers. If a public meeting format is adopted, it is important to remember that people with learning disabilities will require extra help by way of transport and support staff in order to ensure that they have equality of access.

Accessible information

If people with learning disabilities and carers are to prepare themselves appropriately prior to meetings and participate in the same way as other Board members, agendas, minutes and reports need to be available in accessible formats (Table 3.4). Chairs, and commissioners who sat on Partnership Boards, were often extremely proud of the accessibility of their paperwork, although they were quick to admit that this had been a steep learning curve:

> "I mean it's interesting going back over the paperwork and indeed over the strategies we've produced in that if you start with the earlier

meetings you see they're not at all, not very accessible at all, and the early strategies weren't very accessible, whereas I hope now they're much more accessible." (Chair)

However, the same degree of satisfaction was not always reflected in the opinions of other Board members. People with learning disabilities tended to agree that there had been considerable improvements in the accessibility of information:

> "We have actually been fighting with them to make the information much more accessible. I have had to say that the signs are that they are improving." (Self-advocate)

But they often still had concerns that more needed to be done, as evidenced by the limited availability of audiotapes and of paperwork with pictures or symbols to supplement large-print text.

Table 3.4: Accessible formats used for Partnership Board materials

Nature of accessible format	Available	Not available
Big-print size used	9	1
Jargon-free documents	9	1
Pictures or symbols as well as text	3	7
Audiotapes of documents	3	7[a]

Note: Partnership Boards might use more than one accessible format.

[a] Of these, a further three had been promised that tapes would soon be made available.

Somewhat surprisingly, carers reported at least as much dissatisfaction with Partnership Board information as people with learning disabilities. Many highlighted the unacceptable use of jargon:

> "So much of it is so in jargon. I struggle, but I do feel that I am reasonably intelligent but I sometimes lose the thread of it just by trying to translate the language of it." (Carer)

> "I once spent 20 minutes on the phone trying to find out what these abbreviations meant on a two-sided piece of A4, before I could read it." (Carer)

However, at least an equal number disliked the accessible material produced:

> "I know for a fact that the more user friendly you make it to explain everything, it means a lot more reading, because you are having to use very simple words." (Carer)

> "If you ask me which version I prefer, I prefer the non-accessible version because I'm used to reading that type of thing." (Carer)

As with many other issues relating to the operation of Partnership Boards, opposing pressures and arguments were at work here. A number of Boards had decided, on the basis of equality, that only one – accessible – version of any document would be produced, but this clearly did not please everyone. In the attempt to make information accessible for people with learning disabilities, it is important not to alienate other groups. It may therefore still be necessary to continue to produce some complex documents in both accessible and non-accessible formats.

There is also a question mark over whether all supposedly 'accessible' material is genuinely so. Research shows that accessible information requires not only large print and unambiguous pictures, but also simple language in short sentences, an appropriate format or medium (for example, CD ROM; video) and – most importantly – close partnership working with the intended audience in order to ensure that it is meeting their particular needs. There is no 'one size fits all' way of producing good accessible information, but there is now a strong evidence base and clear guidance from which to work (Townsley et al, 2003; Rodgers et al, 2004). Partnership Boards need to be in the vanguard of promoting best practice in this area, not simply continuing with something that may not, in fact, be meeting the needs of Board members. Mechanisms therefore need to be in place to check whether 'accessible' outputs are genuinely accessible to their intended audience.

Whatever the format, all information needs to be produced and circulated in plenty of time. Partnership Board members – both self-advocates and carers – frequently reported unacceptable delays in the circulation of minutes and agendas. This impaired not only upon their ability to consult effectively with others, but also their own ability to participate in meetings:

"In the early days we never even got information prior to the meetings and so you went to the Partnership Board and really you just couldn't get involved." (Carer)

Accessible and timely information is an indispensable requirement of successful partnership. Only through access to information can people with learning disabilities and carers seek to influence the decisions that will affect their lives.

Good practice checklist 6
Accessible information

Information should be available

- In large print size.
- With pictures or symbols as well as text.
- Avoiding jargon and acronyms.
- Using simple language in short sentences.
- On audiotapes for people with visual impairments and others who prefer information on tape.

Remember

- Sometimes more detailed information will be required than is possible to include in a brief, accessible report.
- It is not necessarily 'bad practice' to produce accessible *and* 'non-accessible' versions of a document.
- Producing documents on time can be as important as producing them in accessible formats.

  See Rodgers et al (2004) for guidance on producing accessible information in different formats.

three

Commissioning and managing for strategic change

Introduction

Within the public sector, service commissioning is a relatively new role. It began in earnest under the Thatcher government, with the move towards contracting out publicly-funded services to independent sector providers. In the case of social care services, this trend was formalised by the 1990 NHS and Community Care Act, which required that a significant proportion of local authority social care services be contracted out to the independent sector rather than provided in-house as before (Lewis and Glennerster, 1996). Since this time, commissioners have played a key role in learning disability services (and, indeed, in other areas of health and social care). This role (DH, 2001a) is to focus on the need of service users and carers; to gather information about populations and need; to engage in strategic planning to build capacity; and to do so while demonstrating effective joint working.

For learning disability services, the legacy of the 1980s and 1990s in many parts of the country has been the replacement of large, publicly-owned institutions ('mental handicap' hospitals) on the edge of towns with many smaller, privately run mini-institutions (residential care homes)

scattered throughout towns and countryside. Although these changes could be said to have resulted in greater physical integration of people with learning disabilities, effective support to enable people to become socially integrated within their local communities (as envisaged by *Valuing People*) has been less common. And there is little to suggest that people with learning disabilities are, as yet, actively involved in purchasing and commissioning the services they require (Simons, 1999).

More recently, some independent and voluntary sector service providers have sought to embrace the concept of person centredness and, as a result, have begun to offer a wider range of services, including supported living packages and 'building free' day services. Other providers, however, have not yet begun to change their mode of operation and appear unlikely to do so unless significant pressures are brought to bear upon them. Since independent-sector care services are, essentially, businesses, this pressure can most readily be exerted through market forces. At its most basic, this means that service commissioners would stop purchasing services that are not person-centred; as a result, providers that failed to

four

offer person-centred services would eventually go out of business.

In practice, of course, changing patterns of purchasing is far from simple. It requires not only the active development of local markets in social care but also effective quality-assurance mechanisms (see, for example, Bliss et al, 1999) to ensure that service users really are exerting control over their own lives. In directly provided services, senior managers can use a variety of tools, including staff training, stakeholder events and the development of new types of services, to promote the person-centred approaches demanded by *Valuing People*. By contrast, where services have been contracted out to independent or voluntary sector providers, changes must be brought about through working in partnership with provider organisations and by amendments to future contracting agreements.

This chapter examines a number of important aspects of the role of commissioners in implementing the provisions of the White Paper, drawing on a variety of data sources from the study. It explores in turn:

- the relationship between commissioning and care management;
- the commissioners' role in shaping local markets in care provision;
- their operational role in supporting the process of change management within directly provided and contracted-out services; and
- their own training and professional development needs.

Commissioning and care management

Engaging *proactively* with providers of social care services is crucial for commissioning person-centred services. Rather than simply reacting to local independent providers by purchasing or not purchasing a particular service, commissioners must increasingly use their skills and knowledge either to help new and existing provider organisations to develop in the right direction or to attract organisations that are providing person-centred services elsewhere into their area.

Both commissioners and care managers have crucial roles to play in creating an environment where individual, person-centred packages of support become the norm rather than the exception, if the aspirations of the White Paper are to be realised. However, the state of affairs described here by one commissioner is certainly not unique to their local authority:

> "There is definitely a monopoly of large residential providers and in the past we've played to that because I think the way we've commissioned services has tended to be in a crisis, on a Friday afternoon and they've been there with the residential bed."

This situation has in part been created by past failures on the part of both care managers and commissioners to work proactively. Care managers have failed to assess need in such a way as to pre-empt a crisis and commissioners have failed to develop local markets in more innovative packages of support.

Care management (as introduced by the 1990 NHS and Community Care Act) was intended, among other things, to provide a means of directly linking needs assessment to the creation of *individualised* packages of care. In practice, what appears to have happened in some areas is that care managers have become assessors and administrators (Ramcharan et al, 1999) who then purchase standard 'care products', most commonly places in residential care homes and traditional day centres. The commissioners interviewed as part of this study were frequently critical of this formulaic approach to care management:

> "They think care management is about a menu in the sense of which home can we find that's the cheapest." (Commissioner)

> "Because we haven't got enough care managers, there is still some core practice where you'll get individual care management practitioners who say: *this person needs day care, full stop*. We still find that." (Commissioner)

Such criticisms of care managers are, perhaps, rather unfair. Care managers are often caught between a desire to find person-centred packages of support and the necessity of keeping costs within budget. Added to these limitations is the fact that they can purchase only those services that are available, without the remit to lobby for change or develop new services:

> "If the care managers haven't got the suppliers then clearly they can't commission [purchase], and if you look at the track record of learning disability services, in the end the innovation has always come either from family carers or from service providers, never particularly from care management." (Commissioner)

The role of care managers is largely concerned with assessment of need against agreed criteria. How these needs are then met will depend on what services are available; and it is largely down to commissioners to ensure that non-standard packages of support are available for care managers to choose from in line with the goals of the White Paper. What remains the responsibility of care managers, however, is to develop their practice so that needs assessment becomes a proactive monitoring of changing needs and wishes rather than a one-off event (Cambridge, 1999). If effective, such systems can make it more likely that their purchasing of services happens in a planned manner rather than in response to a crisis.

Care managers and commissioners need to work closely together to build effective information databases about the needs of local populations as well as individuals (Russell, 2001). Without such information, commissioners cannot hope to know what types or amounts of services they need to commission. One of the dangers of person-centred approaches is that *everything* is reduced to a purely individual perspective. But it is only by responding to needs at a *population* level that services can be commissioned that maximise flexibility within limited resources. In the

four

absence of such an approach, there is a real risk that innovative and individualised support services will only ever become available to those people with the most active and influential advocates or circles of support. This leaves people with learning disabilities who have few family or community ties in real danger of receiving second-rate services and perhaps remaining trapped in residential care because care management alone is not sufficiently proactive to ensure a better outcome for them.

Developing and managing local markets in care

Care managers can offer people with learning disabilities access only to those services that are available in the local market, that is to say, those services that have been commissioned. In some parts of the country, independent and voluntary sector providers are in the vanguard of change, working closely with service users and commissioners to develop person-centred services. However, this is not the case everywhere, nor are all independent sector providers innovative and forward-thinking. Commissioners must therefore seek to influence the services that become available through exercising what powers they have.

Good practice checklist 7
Care management and service commissioning

Care management and service commissioning

- How often are individual needs assessed? Assessment should take place not only in response to a crisis but as part of a rolling programme.
- Assessments should detail both current and future needs and wishes. Future needs might include predictable changes in circumstance due to – for example – family carers getting older, or individuals' express desire for changes in their support package.
- Information about assessed need should be recorded in such a way that it can be used to help plan future services. This means using a computerised system from which data can easily be extracted. For example, an effective system should be able to draw out information on the number of people with carers aged over 65, or the number of young adults in need of housing.
- Care managers and commissioners need to develop effective channels of communication. Even the best information system will not be able to identify all trends in future demand for services. Care managers needs to regularly update commissioners about what new services they believe are needed; likewise, commissioners must keep care managers informed of plans for the future development of services so that they can offer every available option to service users.
- Care managers should be encouraged to identify service shortfalls and to systematically record them.

Commissioners interviewed for this study suggested a number of tactics for managing local markets in care.

Regardless of how a contract is awarded, the *type* of contract used is crucial to determining the relationship between commissioners and providers of services. Other authors have discussed how commissioners can use the contracting process to ensure that the service principles they espouse are enshrined in the practice of provider organisations (Brown and Cambridge, 1995; Cambridge and Brown, 1997). Evidence from our study demonstrated that most local authorities are currently moving away from 'block' contracts, in which a number of residential beds or day-service placements are purchased from a provider which must then be filled, to 'spot' contracts, in which services are purchased individually after a comprehensive local assessment of need has been undertaken.

> "Looking at the pattern, the last few years it looks like it's mostly been spot contracts. There's a few block contracts we hold, but they basically originate from the last set of long-stay closures – from 10 years ago." (Commissioner)

On the face of it, spot contracts should enable the development of services that are person-centred, since each contract can be written to reflect the particular needs and wishes of an individual. In practice, the issue is complicated by the fact that spot contracts may, in a business sense, make the

four

Good practice checklist 8
Managing local care markets

Building local capacity and ensuring service quality in contracted-out services

- Ask for broad 'expressions of interest' and let providers come up with innovative service designs, rather than tendering to a narrow, pre-determined specification.
- Arrange meetings with providers to ask what services they might be interested in developing.
- Invite well-respected provider organisations that do not currently operate in your area to tender for new services.
- Offer financial incentives to smaller providers to help them change to new ways of working.
- Look for good examples of person-centred services elsewhere in the country and ask local providers to emulate these approaches.
- Accept that, as businesses, providers will need to be guaranteed minimum contracts (by length of time and volume of service) in order to make it worth their while investing in change.
- Make sure quality assurance measures are in place. Use this system to check whether contractual obligations are being met in full.
- If provider organisations are unable or unwilling to change, then make it clear that in the longer-term their contracts may not be renewed.

development of new services *more* difficult than block contracts, because spot contracts do not provide the same degree of income guarantee for provider organisations. In economic terms, the use of spot contracts shifts the financial risk from the local authority to the service provider. Since businesses will tend to try to minimise such risks to their future income, a complete move to spot contracting may make it difficult to maintain relationships with existing providers or to attract new providers into an area.

A variety of solutions to the problems thrown up by spot contracting were revealed by commissioners interviewed in this research. All of these were designed to make the provision of person-centred services a viable business proposition for provider organisations, without at the same time the paramount importance of the service user's needs and wishes being lost from view.

Void agreements

In order to encourage/enable providers to move to spot contracts, it was sometimes possible to come to an agreement about sharing the financial risks:

> "We've avoided blocks and we've worked with our provider partners to come to arrangements about things like voids periods – to try and cushion some of the impact of not having blocks. I don't think we've been overly generous but we've not been unreasonable." (Commissioner)

This type of arrangement should, perhaps, be considered only where commissioners are confident that the service provider is offering the kinds of support that people with learning disabilities want. So, for example, this arrangement might be used for a supported living service, but not automatically adopted with every provider of residential care homes.

'Cost and volume' contracts

This type of contract is a half-way house between block and spot contracting and as such may offer benefits to both commissioners and providers. The contract agrees that an amount of service that varies between specified minimum and maximum levels will be purchased over an agreed period of time. For commissioners, this offers greater flexibility and responsiveness than block contracts, while offering providers more financial security than spot contracting. One commissioner summed up the benefits thus:

> "We have stability because we can pick and choose, but the providers have a bit more stability about where they're going.... The cost and volume contract will probably be for three years or something like that. Because I know, from a commissioner point of view, that if a provider is no good then there's a legal framework to actually stop them having the contract anyway, regardless of whether it's spot, block, or cost and volume. But the flip side is, from a purchasing point of view, it gives them more stability to then plan their services better."

Enabling provider organisations to plan future service developments with confidence is crucial to the development of local markets. Giving providers a greater degree of financial security enables them to plan and develop new, more person-centred services.

Minimum guarantees of business

Essentially a variation on 'cost and volume' contracts, this type of agreement may be particularly useful for the development of supported living services. At its core, the contract would say, as one commissioner put it:

> "We can guarantee you a minimum amount of business, but which individuals you're supporting and the exact number of people and the exact hours will vary over time."

Although *spot contracts* can provide a responsive and flexible way of meeting individual needs, they can make it harder for commissioners to maintain a clear grasp of the wider picture:

> "It's all been individually spot-contracted, I think that's great; it has been person-centred. But on the other hand we haven't perhaps looked at emerging themes coming through." (Commissioner)

Such a problem is not an argument against the use of spot contracting arrangements but a reminder that commissioners have to seek to balance the competing demands of meeting needs on an individual basis and retaining a clear sense of the strategic development of services for the population at large. This is yet another reason why effective information systems and good communication between commissioners and care managers is crucial. Effective strategies cannot simply be created by aggregating the results of individual person-centred plans; but having a sense of the types of services desired by people with learning disabilities should enable commissioners to commission services that reflect and respond to individual wants and needs.

Where *block contracts* remain, they *can* be made responsive to individual needs if they include sufficient detail about the type and quality of support to be provided to each person. The same, of course, is true of both spot and cost-and-volume contracts. In all types of contracting, the small print is important. The points in the following checklist were all suggested by commissioners as vital components of contracts, in order to ensure the quality of housing and support provided.

Contracting arrangements are a fairly blunt instrument with which to seek to bring about change within services for people with learning disabilities. They may be a *necessary* precondition for fundamental changes to the types of support services available, but they are unlikely ever to be *sufficient* in themselves to ensure that services become truly person-centred. Changes to contracts must be complemented with an effective programme of change management that seeks to affect both culture and practice within statutory and independent and voluntary sector services.

four

Good practice checklist 9
Contracting 'small print'

As minimum requirements, all contracts should stipulate that:
- Each person will have an individual care plan in place, to be updated regularly with full involvement of the individual concerned.
- Each person who so wishes will be supported to develop their own person-centred plan.
- Each person will have regular medical checks; this will include their GP, dentist, optician, audiologist, and so forth.
- A minimum proportion of support staff must be trained in accordance with the Learning Disability Awards Framework (LDAF) qualification.

Change management

Many commissioners, particularly those whose role included a significant degree of operational responsibility, expressed strong opinions about the current agenda for change. Some, perhaps inevitably, were concerned about the sheer volume of changes being undertaken simultaneously:

> "One of the problems in terms of the whole delivery of the government's agenda is that there's just so much change, and so many targets, and improvement plans, and whatever." (Commissioner)

Others preferred to emphasise the concept not of 'change' but of 'service improvement':

> "I actually have a problem with the word 'change', because there's clearly changes around us, it's absolutely a constant. So what are learning disability managers all about? They are about improving services; not just changing. Improving services and improving people's lives. And clearly that's

what *Valuing People* is about." (Commissioner)

There was, however, near-unanimous agreement among commissioners both that change was necessary – and that the kind of changes required in learning disability services was as much about shifting individual attitudes and organisational culture as about restructuring or introducing new policies and procedures. This emphasis on the need for cultural change within learning disability services echoes the messages that have emanated from the Valuing People Support Team (Greig, 2003). In this context, most commissioners regarded it as imperative not only that the thrust of cultural change should be towards more person-centred approaches but also that:

> "People with the learning difficulties and carers feel that they are having a say. They're listened to. They're driving the change with us." (Commissioner)

However, beyond involvement in Partnership Boards, there was little evidence to suggest that service users, self-advocates or carers were in any way actively involved in the commissioning process.

Various approaches to change management were evident among the commissioners interviewed. Techniques suggested by them for ensuring that new attitudes were embraced by staff at all levels, and across the statutory and non-statutory sectors, included the following ideas, each of which is illustrated with a direct quotation from an interview.

Reflect on practice; learn from elsewhere

"For me I think probably one of the crucial bits about change is about reflective practice in terms of getting people to think through what works OK and what doesn't, and also getting people to look at things outside their own areas; so getting people to come in and basically explain and look at what's going on to help us think things through." (Commissioner)

Decide where you want to go and how to get there

"Get people to think through where we want to be in so many years time, and then to say, well what are we going to do to get there? Who needs to be involved? And whilst that isn't a change technique in itself, it does help to visualise what needs to happen." (Commissioner)

Constantly repeat values to help inculcate them into practice

"We did make a conscious decision within the management team that the *Nothing about us without us* logo would be used [this is the title of the report from the Service Users Advisory Group, 2001] and we would bandy that around so that people had a sort of fairly catchy thing that was easy to remember and so it was deliberately promoted." (Commissioner)

Explain why change is taking place as well as the direction it is taking

"I think ensuring that people are engaged in that change process is very, very important. So it's enabling staff to have the information to understand why change is necessary and why the development of an organisation is going down a certain route." (Commissioner)

Understand why some staff may lack enthusiasm for change ...

"I think what we have met is apathy in certain groups of people who have done this before: *we've done this before and why should that be different?*" (Commissioner)

... but don't accept this as a reason for blocking change

"But then you have to come to a point where you say that really something now has to move

four

forward. The decision has got to be made; the navel gazing has gone on long enough." (Commissioner)

Recognise that change must go beyond specialist services

"I think the biggest agenda, is how we work with society.... We want individuals with learning disability to be mainstreamed and not socially excluded. So how do we ensure that local communities include people with learning disabilities?" (Commissioner)

Accept that change may sometimes be a slow process ...

"It's not about an instant change. If there were instant changes I'd be really anxious because I don't actually think they're sustainable and I think that's going to create a bigger problem for us later on." (Commissioner)

... but positive results can be achieved

"Some key players left willingly and then I changed the management structure and I changed the way we thought about things and then people shifted. It was amazing, you had the tip and we tipped and the last 12 months we've been running." (Commissioner)

Good practice checklist 10
Valuing People and change

Change should:
- be based on the promotion of *Valuing People*'s core principles of rights, choice, independence and social inclusion;
- be owned by people with learning disabilities, their families and advocates;
- be overseen by the Partnership Board;
- involve both statutory and independent/voluntary sector organisations;
- seek to change organisational culture as well as practice; involve all staff, from senior managers to front-line support workers; seek to engage with generic services, so that they also come to understand and share the core principles of *Valuing People*;
- seek to engage with the local community as much as possible; be an ongoing process through which practice is questioned and improved rather than a one-off event;
- take due account of the fears that some people with learning disabilities, their carers (and staff) may have about changes to patterns of support, particularly if they have previously had negative experiences of change;
- and not be undertaken for its own sake but in order to improve services and empower service users.

Commissioners' training and professional development needs

Commissioners of services for people with learning disabilities are a hugely diverse group. Those in our study had come to the job from a wide variety of professional backgrounds, including social work, nursing, clinical psychology and the voluntary and independent sectors. The job of commissioning also varied significantly from local authority to local authority, dividing broadly between those posts that did, and those that did not, include significant operational management responsibilities in addition to the commissioning role.

The fact that commissioning is a relatively new role and may encompass a wide range of different job specifications poses some unique difficulties, not least in determining the qualities and qualifications necessary to do the job well. There are currently no formal, nationally recognised qualifications that relate exclusively to the commissioning role, let alone the specifics of commissioning services for people with learning disabilities. A number of commissioners in the study held management qualifications, such as MBAs, but an MBA is neither an automatic prerequisite for the job nor one likely to fulfil all of a commissioner's training requirements.

In the two years prior to the publication of *Valuing People*, two training and development consultancy organisations in learning disability, the National Development Team and Paradigm UK, jointly ran national training programmes that were specifically designed to promote better commissioning. In a series of two-day events, participants were given the opportunity to question the value base of their commissioning practice and to ask whether or how this needed to change. They were also exposed to a broad range of innovative ideas for future service development, including non-traditional housing and day-service options; supported employment; person-centred planning and circles of support; and new ways of funding services, including the use of direct payments.

Those who had taught on this course indicated in research interviews that they had attempted to emphasise the need for commissioners to work in partnership with provider organisations in order to develop new kinds of support services. Feedback from participants at the time had generally been positive, and in some cases course participants had contacted tutors in order to get more specific advice on implementing changes to their local services.

What difference had the course made to those who had participated in it?

Those interviewed as part of the study cited the following main benefits:

- gaining a broader understanding of the commissioning role;
- exposure to new ideas;
- opportunity to network with other commissioners;
- time away from the office to do 'blue skies' thinking;
- direct contact with experts in various fields; and

four

- inspiration to change and improve local services.

There were, however, also some criticisms. Some commissioners said that they wanted more than 'just' inspirational talk; they wanted concrete examples of *what* to do and *how* to do it. At the same time, however, when specific examples of successful change *were* presented, fears were expressed that these were the achievements of singular, charismatic individuals, and as such could not be replicated elsewhere. These two contradictory points of view capture an important paradox: the set of circumstances that enabled one commissioner, working in a local authority at a specific moment in time, to push services in a particular direction, might never recur. Those circumstances were created by the confluence of pre-existing patterns of local service provision, national and local policies, the dynamism and innovation of local provider organisations and the vision of key stakeholders. Any attempt to recreate the same result, using the same mechanisms but in another authority at another moment in time, might well fail. What can succeed, however, is *adapting* a previously successful blueprint to fit new, and different, local circumstances.

An alternative means for commissioners to share both problems and good practice has been the *action learning sets* established by the *Valuing People* Support Team as forums for debate and problem solving. Of those commissioners who had taken part in action learning sets, most were enthusiastic about the kind of support and networking opportunities they provided. Those

commissioners who were less certain about the value of spending their time in such a way tended to report that their group had been poorly attended. It would appear that in commissioner development, as in so many other aspects of commissioning, partnership approaches give the most positive results for all participants.

To conclude, commissioners in different parts of the country were often at very different stages of implementing *Valuing People*. For some the White Paper came as little more than a welcome government endorsement of the direction in which their services were already developing. For others, however, the change agenda was daunting in its size and scope. Coming together with other commissioners to share knowledge and experience, whether through action learning sets or other training, is a (relatively) cheap and effective way of developing commissioners' skills. Commissioners can glean valuable ideas for innovative services from service providers, but other commissioners are often best placed to offer up-to-date advice on wider aspects of the commissioning role.

Changing support, enabling choice and independence

Introduction

Valuing People sets out a number of challenges for local services that must be met if its aspirations of social inclusion for people with learning disabilities are to be achieved. Key cornerstones for changing support and enabling choice and independence are seen to be: person-centred planning, increased housing options, modernisation of day services and more access to employment opportunities.

In this chapter, key issues and debates relating to these areas that were highlighted through the research are presented. These debates are important in determining the principles that underpin strategic plans. If changes are to be made to the ways in which support is offered to people with learning disabilities, then the philosophical and the practical need to be in harmony. Without constant referral back to core principles, practice may be distorted by budgetary pressures or brought to a halt by the inertia of existing systems. Without plausible means of putting these principles into practice, even the most laudable philosophies become meaningless.

Implementing any policy or operationalising any principle is hard work. People with learning disabilities, their families and friends, frontline and senior staff in both statutory and non-statutory sectors need to work together to create changes in both culture and practice. Many people (as noted earlier) harbour very real fears about the effect that any proposed changes may have upon their lives. Many may have had – negative – experiences of change: change in which they had little or no say; change that had unwanted consequences. This is not to argue against change per se but simply to recall that plans for positive change need to be carefully thought through.

What follows is drawn from the hopes, fears and dilemmas expressed by the commissioners of learning disability services who were involved in our research. Some examples of good practice are included but a prescriptive 'how to' approach is avoided. This research has explored the change *process* rather than its *outcomes*. Some of the examples provided may inspire readers to try new approaches; *Appendix A* provides details of a number of further sources of information and advice. Detailed papers on each of the topics, prepared for the expert seminars organised as part of the study, can also be downloaded from the project's Strategies for Change website (see *Appendix A*).

Person-centred planning

A person-centred approach to planning means that planning

should start with the individual (not with services) and take account of their wishes and aspirations. Person-centred planning is a mechanism for reflecting the needs and wishes of a person with a learning disability and covers such issues as housing, education, employment and leisure. (DH, 2001b, para 4.17)

Person-centred planning (PCP) has, in a sense, become *the* mantra for learning disability services for the new millennium. In many respects this is to be welcomed. Few would argue against the idea that the needs and aspirations of people should come before the convenience of services; that people with learning disabilities should be included in the mainstream of society with respect to housing, employment, leisure and other opportunities; and that, in order for these aspirations to become a reality, both specialist and generic services need to radically alter their approach to providing support.

Some commentators, however, are concerned that attempts to 'do' person-centredness too quickly will lose its radical, empowering essence, and person-centred planning may become little more than another social service process for assessing need and allocating resources (O'Brien and Towell, 2004). Even where this trap is avoided, other potential pitfalls are feared. What are the equity implications if this becomes the standard model for service delivery? That is, how can we ensure that those people without strong supporters are given the same opportunities and access to resources as those with more powerful

social networks and advocacy to draw upon?

If person-centred approaches and person-centred planning processes are to be embraced effectively, then it seems from our research that the following issues and questions need to be discussed with local stakeholders.

Which comes first: the plan or the approach?

Some commissioners interviewed as part of this research were uncertain about the possibility of working in a person-centred *way* until individuals in the area had got a person-centred *plan*:

> "We can't work in a person-centred way to support people if people haven't got a person-centred plan."

A person-centred plan is clearly a very useful tool through which to support radical change in a person's life; but the absence of individual plans should not preclude support services from ensuring that *their* approach is person-centred. As another commissioner put it:

> "How do you change the way somebody lives their life if you don't put the services in place in the first place? So you've got to have housing in place, you've got to have employment, access to further education, and so on."

Person-centred planning and a person-centred approach need to go hand in hand. If person-centred planning is to become a process that is accessible to — and transforming for – every person with a learning disability, radical changes to the types and amounts of services on offer will undoubtedly be required. However, waiting for services to change may mean waiting for a long time.

In the meantime, pioneers are needed in order to create a positive cycle of change. If a few individuals develop person-centred plans, whose implementation of which challenges traditional models of support and proves that alternatives are achievable, then this will both encourage service providers to change the types of support they offer and show other people with learning disabilities that different lifestyles are possible. This approach has been *proven* to work for individuals (Sanderson et al, 2002) and an increasing body of evidence-based advice for managers and commissioners shows how principles can be put into practice more broadly (Cole et al, 2000; McIntosh and Whittaker, 2000). (For information on the research project on person-centred planning, funded by the Department of Health and due to report in 2005, see the Foundation for People with Learning Disabilities' website, *Appendix A*.)

How does person-centred planning fit with strategic planning?

The relationship between person-centred planning and strategic planning is not straightforward. *Person-centred planning* is essential to create individualised packages of support that enable people to fulfil their wishes and dreams beyond the statutory services. In order to enable such a reality to become commonplace, *strategic plans* need to be angled towards the

development of flexible support services responsive to individual needs and wishes.

Commissioners in the study were aware that strategic plans needed to be informed by the data from individual plans on the kinds of support wanted – but that the risk of institutionalising person-centred planning in the process had to be avoided. As one commissioner commented:

> "What we don't want to do is turn PCP into a numbers game, and turn it into a process of, well you're doing that because it needs to inform this [strategic plan]. Fundamentally PCP, as you will know, is about the individual, so we're going to think through how we get information off that without putting undue pressure on people to conform to it."

The Centre for Inclusive Futures has recently undertaken a series of workshops, involving people with learning disabilities, their families and supporters, as well as service providers and academics, to examine the dynamics between person-centred and strategic planning. The resulting papers (O'Brien and Towell, 2003, 2004) can be downloaded from the Strategies for Change website (see *Appendix A* for details).

How does person-centred planning fit with care management?

If person-centred planning is to have maximum impact, then services need to be clear about the differences between person-centred planning and care

five

management. For some commissioners it was unclear how they fitted together:

> "Person-centred planning doesn't really follow the care management process at the moment; and it should do."

Care management and person-centred planning need to act in tandem while remaining separate processes with separate goals. *Care management* is about assessing need against an agreed set of standard criteria in order to determine whether or not a particular individual is entitled to receive certain amounts of support. Care management rightly acts as a gatekeeper to those monies and services that are provided through the public purse. As one commissioner said:

> "I've got no objection to care management, but I still see it as an organisational tool rather than an individual tool."

Person-centred planning, on the other hand, takes a much broader approach that looks at all aspects of a person's life and aspirations, not just those elements of need that might be met by statutory services (DH, 2002b). Care management might adopt a person-centred approach and seek innovative, individualised solutions rather than relying upon traditional packages of care, but it can never provide for all the different needs and wishes of every individual.

Sometimes person-centred planning may offer people with learning disabilities a way of setting out how they wish their 'statutory needs' to be met. It may also, as

one commissioner suggested, be used as evidence to justify why a particular individual needs certain services:

> "One of the things that I keep panicking people over is, if a service is beyond a certain amount of money we should really be saying, well we need to have a person-centred plan to think through why we're going in that direction. I also think it would make people think a bit more creatively as well."

But there are always likely to be significant elements of a person-centred plan – for example, a foreign holiday; hot air ballooning; going to listen to a pop star – that are not the responsibility of statutory social or health services to meet but which may be realised through other means, like an individual's circle of support or other social networks (discussed later). These are the elements of a person-centred plan which should become increasingly important if the inclusive lifestyles aspired to in *Valuing People* are to become a reality for people with learning disabilities: elements which are not part of the business of services and which they should not seek to control.

Who should support person-centred planning work?

There was uncertainty among some commissioners about where the responsibility for person-centred planning should lie. One commissioner, for example, said:

> "I'm still not entirely convinced that workers in a community team

are the best people to be doing person-centred planning, because of some of the tensions that quite rightly arise. And perhaps they're not challenging enough."

The consensus in organisations such as Circles Network (see *Appendix A*) is that a person-centred plan should not be 'owned' by anyone other than the individual who is at the centre of the process and those close to him or her (Sanderson et al, 1997). People with learning disabilities should be able to decide who they wish to be involved in their person-centred plans; this may or may not include members of community learning disability teams or other services. If part of the person's plans require the support of statutory services, at least in the sense of providing financial resources, then involvement of people from community teams becomes inevitable. But members of the community team should not seek to take over the process. Some commissioners were aware that this did not always sit easily with colleagues in statutory services:

> "There does still seem to be this …
> the way best way I can describe it is
> like, this kind of, like, benign
> paternalism, mostly from the
> statutory sector: person-centred
> planning is fine but at the end of
> the day, we're the flagship service,
> we're the people who are most
> highly qualified, highly trained …
> and it seems, to me, to be slightly
> incongruous with the whole idea of
> personal centred planning."
> (Commissioner)

Where a person with a learning disability does not have family members or other friends willing and able to support them, the guidance on person-centred planning makes clear that a nurse, social worker or other community team member could take on a more proactive supporting role (DH, 2002a). Paid workers will, of necessity, have to take on such roles sometimes if person-centred planning is to become a reality for people with little in the way of social support networks. In this case particular care has to be taken to ensure that staff feel able, when necessary, to challenge prevailing service orthodoxies despite the conflicts of interest this might present them with.

Some commissioners were clear that person-centred planning was not something in which statutory services were best placed to be involved. They felt that individuals or groups at arm's length from statutory services should provide the support needed by individuals wishing to develop their own person-centred plan:

> "We're really selling that concept to
> the council: person-centred
> planning we shouldn't touch with a
> bargepole, we should just give
> money to others to do it."

What about people living in private care homes?

As all types of support service are increasingly provided at arm's length from local authorities (Arblaster et al, 1998) person-centred approaches need to be understood and embraced by staff in the independent and voluntary sectors as well

five

as those employed directly by health and social services. Some commissioners were concerned at how this was going to be achieved:

> "How are we going to move to a situation where all those staff, including private sector residential care staff, are involved in community connections-type work and how people can access the mainstream in terms of services, helping people get a life outside learning disability services? And that's what person-centred approach is all about."

Ideas from the research for ensuring that this happens included making training available to staff from all sectors and building person-centredness into contracts. In the longer term, fewer people with learning disabilities may choose to live in residential care environments. In the meantime, there is no reason why such establishments should not seek to provide support in ways that are more socially inclusive and person-centred than at present, in line with the White Paper's requirements. Contracts, although a crude tool, can be used to stipulate minimum requirements in terms of social activities and opportunities outside the home, to enhance opportunities for social integration (see *Chapter 4* for more on this topic).

Can person-centredness be taught?

For commissioners the issue of how to *implement* the person-centred approaches recommended by the White Paper was a real one. Was this something that could be taught? And, if so, how? Perhaps not surprisingly some commissioners reported that certain staff, whether frontline support workers or senior managers, seem to grasp the concept of person-centredness more readily than others. One commissioner, for example, said of a colleague:

> "You could see the way he was working, he was the epitome of personal centredness; you can't teach people that."

Nevertheless, staff *can* be given an understanding of the concept and taught to develop working practices that are in accordance with person-centred approaches. Some commissioners were investing heavily in introducing both staff and service users to person-centred planning:

> "We've spent, over the last 12–18 months, in excess of £12,000 on training. We're going to spend another six or eight grand by the summer on doing some more work around training the trainers, interlinking it with stuff like about accessible information and the use of the Change picture bank.... All the training we've done has been inclusive. Some of the people who can now train people are people who use services."

Person-centredness is not rocket science; its key message is simply to remember that people with learning disabilities are people first, with the same diverse range of hopes, fears, and dreams as everyone else. A range of resources are available to help services, commissioners and others here including the Department of Health's own guidance on the issue (DH, 2002b; see also *Appendix A*: Circles Network and Foundation for People with Learning Disabilities).

We're already person-centred ...

For some commissioners the challenge presented by person-centredness was perceived as minimal:

> "I think, in fairness, [both] external provision and in-house have always had a kind of person-centred approach, or tried as much as is possible to have one. So when the person-centred agenda came on the scene with *Valuing People* we didn't have to shift hugely."

But, given the virtual impossibility of *all* services in any given local authority area being genuinely person-centred for *every* person with learning disability living there at the time that the research took place, might such a statement represent a fundamental misunderstanding of what constitutes a person-centred approach to service delivery and how person-centred planning can empower people with learning disabilities to move beyond 'service land' to lead more fulfilling and socially included lives? Admitting that cultural and practical changes are needed is the first step towards achieving the goal of truly person-centred services.

Creating truly person-centred services will be a long, slow process for many local authorities, as many commissioners frankly admitted. In the meantime they were clear that change should be urged forward as rapidly as possible, but not to the extent

that person-centredness becomes simply another buzzword at the expense of genuine empowerment. As one commissioner put it:

> "It's better to make it real for a smaller number of people than do it for its own sake for a larger number of people."

Housing

> People with learning disabilities can live successfully in different types of housing, from individual self-contained properties, housing networks, group homes, and shared accommodation schemes, through to village and other forms of intentional community. They can cope with the full range of tenures, including home ownership. Expanding the range and choice of housing, care and support services is key to giving individuals more choice and control over their lives. (DH, 2001b, para 7.2)

Where and with whom people live can be viewed as providing a rough and ready indicator of their social status. Historically, people with learning disabilities have – quite literally – lived at the margins of society. More recently the closure of long-stay hospitals has led to greater geographical integration, but in many cases this has yet to translate into true social inclusion.

Person-centredness demands that individuals with learning disabilities be given real choice about where and with

five

whom they live. Changing housing and support services to reflect a wider range of options is perhaps the most difficult task facing learning disability professionals. The difficulties arise from a number of factors, including:

- funding being 'locked up' in existing provision;
- much accommodation being provided by independent sector providers who may fear that change will lead to a collapse in their economic/financial viability; and
- a general shortage of affordable housing in many parts of the country.

Many commissioners reported that they:

> "Struggled to get the housing right because of capacity and because we've got pressures on our budget."

In much the same way that person-centredness has become *the* key concept to define desirable service culture, the 'buzzword' in housing is becoming 'supported living'. There is a danger, however, that this is beginning to be a phrase that means all things to all people.

At its best, supported living denotes a truly person-centred approach to meeting an individual's housing and support needs. An individual will have his or her own home, a tenancy agreement, and support, as required, to maintain the tenancy and to develop a socially inclusive lifestyle (Simons and Ward, 1997; Simons, 2000). Schemes such as KeyRing, which uses volunteers to support small networks of people with learning disabilities, all of whom live in their own homes and are in

walking distance of one another, are a prime exemplar of such ideals (Simons, 1998b).

Supporting People

One factor behind the recent rise in supported living arrangements has undoubtedly been implementation of *Supporting People* (DETR, 2001). This is the government's programme for providing housing-related support to all people who, for whatever reason, need help to retain their housing tenancies and attain or maintain independence. It 'went live' on 1 April 2003 following a lengthy run-in period, during which local authorities sought to identify and rationalise the complex funding streams through which various vulnerable groups received housing-related support (Griffiths, 2000). The programme was underpinned by the desire to separate 'bricks and mortar' housing costs, which will continue to be paid as rent and through housing benefit (if individuals are eligible), from the costs of housing-related support.

Although a broad range of support services may be funded through *Supporting People*, there are also some clear exclusions. Most significantly, for people with learning disabilities, *Supporting People* monies cannot be used to pay for support provided in the context of registered residential accommodation. In the run-up to implementation it appeared that some social service departments were attempting to bypass this rule (and shift costs on to *Supporting People* budgets) by de-registering residential care homes and renaming them 'supported living services'. If done in good faith, that is, to enhance the choice, independence and social inclusion of people with learning disabilities, such moves would be entirely within the spirit of both *Supporting People* and *Valuing People*. But if done for other (perhaps financial) motives, the resulting changes may be of little or no benefit to people with learning disabilities. As one commissioner said:

> "I suspect if you walked into a number of those services at the minute and mapped them against residential care versus supported living values I think you'll have some difficulty in recognising the change."

Managers and commissioners can hardly be blamed for making the most of a new funding stream. Indeed, a number expressed regret at their perceived 'failure to grasp that window of opportunity' offered by the introduction of *Supporting People*. But it should be incumbent upon those who 'took the money' to ensure that the changes are more than just 'name deep'.

Housing and partnership

One thing remains certain: the housing and support needs of all people with learning disabilities will not be met through *Supporting People;* other options must be actively pursued.

As in so many other areas, the key to successful housing strategies for people with learning disabilities lies in developing effective partnerships – in this case partnerships with those individuals and organisations that control access to housing

stock. The following examples of successful partnership working were mentioned by commissioners. They demonstrate a variety of ways in which the housing needs of people with learning disabilities can be met through enabling them to access the same housing options as other members of their local communities, in line with the aspirations of *Valuing People*.

Learning Disability Partnership Boards' housing strategies

Although of sometimes variable quality (Harker and King, 2003; Knight, 2003), the best of the local housing strategies developed by Learning Disability Partnership Boards offered positive examples of effective partnership working. In particular, several commissioners had succeeded – through the Partnership Board – in getting housing services (both statutory and non-statutory), rather than social care services, to take the lead on housing:

> "The housing association appointed a lead who wrote the housing strategy on behalf of us all ... people didn't see it as competitive so the other housing associations all signed up to it; it was signed up to by cabinet, signed up to by the commissioning board."
> (Commissioner)

> "We've got a director of housing on the Partnership Board and they've led, with people with the learning difficulties and carers, some workshops to pull together the housing plan. And it's really

five

powerful because it's been led by a District Council who have the responsibility for mainstream housing and I think that's been very successful." (Commissioner)

Council housing

Building capacity in housing was a huge issue for most commissioners. One avenue for increasing the availability of housing for people with learning disabilities was to lobby to change the systems by which council housing was allocated:

> "People with learning disabilities need to be on the waiting list and allocation policies need to reflect learning disability as being a reasonable priority in terms of point systems." (Commissioner)

In at least one local authority there was evidence that this approach was about to bear fruit:

> "Within the next year, the whole point system is going to be different for people with learning disabilities and also, as well, we're going to have quotas for flats that we can actually use for people with learning disabilities."
> (Commissioner)

Housing associations and registered social landlords

Other commissioners reported success in proactively engaging housing associations and registered social landlords to provide supported living services:

> "We said: 'The whole of the system generally will actually benefit substantially by you working in partnership with us in developing *Supporting People* and supported living schemes'. And I would say every single organisation we talked to signed up to it. I think that's partly because we explained the outcomes would be a benefit to them as well as the people with learning disabilities."

Private rented sector

In some areas, commissioners reported on the important role played by the private sector (often overlooked) in offering additional choices to people with learning disabilities:

> "There's one provider that actually does an innovative thing where they actually get long-term leases from private landlords and then sub-let properties and provide support themselves ... and that's really provided an opportunity for locals to say where they want to live." (Commissioner)

Options such as this could be particularly useful in areas without substantial stocks of either council or housing association properties.

Shared ownership

Shared ownership has typically been used in areas where the rising cost of property has prevented significant numbers of people from entering the housing market. Under shared ownership schemes, an individual gets a mortgage in the usual way, based upon income; the difference between mortgage borrowing and the cost of a property is then made up by the housing association. The owner/tenant will part-own the property and pay rent to the housing association for the part of the property owned by it. Several areas within the research were attempting to develop shared ownership as an option for people with learning disabilities:

> "Our local housing association have tended not to do shared ownership, whereas London and South East ones have, so we were talking about seeing if there's a way we could do some shared ownership.... I'd like us to be able to use the range of housing options that have been developed nationally that probably haven't been developed locally ... definitely haven't been developed for people with learning difficulties, but have with other client groups or in other parts of the county." (Commissioner)

> "The housing consortium bids – that we've never been part of – we've got a commitment that year on year we'll get an option for some of that money as well, that would take us more into the shared ownership arena." (Commissioner)

(For further information on shared ownership and indeed the range of other housing options available for people with learning disabilities see *Appendix A: Housing Options; see also Simons 1995, 2000.*)

New build developments

Only one commissioner reported having been able to establish an agreement about getting the housing needs of people with learning disabilities recognised in new housing developments:

> "We've now got an agreement with our housing department, for any new development, that we'll get some of the money."

However, with recent indications of a major government drive to promote new build in order to alleviate the housing crisis (particularly in the South East), this may increasingly become an option that commissioners need to actively pursue.

Whatever specific housing options are developed for people with learning disabilities, if the aspirations of *Valuing People* are to be realised, housing authorities and mainstream housing providers must recognise that people with learning disabilities are as much their responsibility as any other socially or economically disadvantaged groups. In the short to medium term, social and health services will undoubtedly need to remain key commissioners of housing services. In the longer term, for the vast majority of people with learning disabilities, housing should not be linked to specialist care.

five

Day services and employment

"For decades, services for people with learning disabilities have been heavily reliant on large, often institutional, day centres. These have provided much needed respite for families, but they have made a limited contribution to promoting social inclusion or independence for people with learning disabilities. People with learning disabilities attending them have not had opportunities to develop individual interests or the skills and experience they need in order to move into employment." (DH, 2001b, para 7.21)

There is now clear evidence from research of the benefits of employment for people with learning disabilities (like other people) not only financially but also in terms of enhanced self-esteem and increased social inclusion (Simons, 1998a; Wistow and Schneider, 2003). And many people with learning disabilities have expressed strong preferences for engaging in paid jobs:

> "At least 50% of the people in our day services say they want jobs, they don't want to be at a day service." (Commissioner)

But recent research indicates that day services are not always effective at supporting moves into employment (Beyer et al, 2004). Nonetheless, unless and until all those people with learning disabilities who wish to do so are enabled to lead socially inclusive lives, day services are likely to remain at the heart of the services

provided for many of them (Simons and Watson, 1999). And in trying to become more person-centred and socially inclusive, day services are faced with a delicate balancing act.

Where with housing the 'buzz concept' is supported living, with day services it is 'buildings-free services'. This means that, rather than gathering together large numbers of people with learning disabilities in a single, segregated building, day service workers are expected instead to support people to access generic education and leisure services within the wider local community.

Taken at face value, this idea seems simple enough. In practice, however, changes to day service structures are often the focus of rigorous local campaigns against change and heated debate (as, for example, in the exchanges on the Choice Forum web-based discussion group: see *Appendix A*). At the heart of these disagreements lie a small number of problems to which there is no clear-cut right or wrong solution, but with which service commissioners and others in our study and beyond must wrestle. (See also papers from the expert seminar organised on Modernising Day Services as part of this research: Strategies for Change, *Appendix A*.)

Day services as respite care

Although few would argue against the principle of buildings-free services, in practice, day services currently also function as a vital source of respite for carers of people with learning disabilities who continue to live in the family home. Family carers are often understandably wary of any changes to service patterns that may result in an overall reduction of hours of support, as commissioners commented:

> "Each time we have done something with day services in the past it's been because of cuts of service, and people have lost service."

Although the needs and wishes of people with learning difficulties need to be the focus of local planning for day services and employment opportunities, those of family carers cannot be ignored. Any benefits of proposed changes must be careful weighed. Who gains? Who loses? Loss of service hours may have serious consequences for those people living at home, in terms of the ability of carers to undertake paid employment or have time for non-care activities, for example.

In some areas, commissioners reported it had proved possible for day services to change the types of support or activities they offered *without* reducing the overall hours of care provided. Such a change did not necessarily require increased financial investment:

> "We had three large day centres, two of which are already closed and have gone to small community based settings. And we haven't put any new money in; what we've done is changed how the money was spent." (Commissioner)

But what such changes did – and do – require is a commitment to person-centredness; partnership working with local community leisure and education facilities; and staff willing to work in new ways.

Segregation or social network?

Traditional day services are often criticised for being 'segregated settings'. The underlying philosophy of *Valuing People* and the government's commitment to social inclusion suggest that people with learning disabilities should no longer be separated from the rest of society in such a fashion, but should instead be included within mainstream facilities. As one commissioner said:

> "We need to look at everybody being in the mainstream and using, not buildings to contain people, but using staff to support people to access the mainstream."

This is a compelling argument. On the other hand, the resulting service orthodoxy may conflict with *Valuing People*'s goal of person-centredness. Many people with learning disabilities have strong and enduring friendships with other day centre users, which they wish to maintain. And, without the day centre as a base, the infrastructure to support both friendships and community-based activities is often lacking – particularly for those unable to travel independently (Beart et al, 2001; Reynolds, 2002).

Valuing People recognised that:

> People with learning disabilities are often socially isolated. Helping people sustain friendships is consistently shown as being one of

five

the greatest challenges faced by learning disability services. Good services will help people with learning disabilities develop opportunities to form relationships. (DH, 2001b, para 7.39)

So commissioners need to balance the imperative to modernise day services with that of enabling people to sustain existing relationships and develop new ones. These relationships may or may not be predominantly with other people with learning disabilities. The imperative for services is not to presume to determine the relationships that individuals might wish to form, nor to preclude the maintenance or development of relationships with certain groups of people, whether inadvertently or as part of a belief that certain kinds of relationships are more valuable – and valued – than others.

Accessing continuing education opportunities

Adults with learning disabilities routinely find their life opportunities (particularly in respect of employment) limited by their lack of formal education and/or vocational qualifications, as well as by social and other barriers (Beyer et al, 2004). Access to adult education can open up a range of opportunities. For young people making the transition from school to adult life, colleges of further education are often the first step. But links to paid employment here are often missing (Heslop et al, 2002). One commissioner noted:

"We're doing some specific work around younger people, 16 to 25, who are not coming into our adult training centres and we think are in college on horrible foundation courses. They've learnt to make baked beans for the last three years and that's what they keep doing, but [we want to know] how we get them onto qualification courses so they can get jobs."

Better communication and partnership working are a vital part of the answer (Heslop et al, 2002). (For information on strategies for making the transition from education to employment, see Jacobsen, 2002 and the website for the National Institute of Adult Continuing Education [NIACE], listed in *Appendix A*.)

Further education is not just about qualifications and employment. Local adult education classes also offer a wide range of activities for people with learning disabilities, ranging from basic literacy and numeracy classes through to more leisure-oriented arts or sporting activities (Sutcliffe, 1996; Sutcliffe and Jacobsen, 1998). Such classes may be developed specifically to meet the needs of people with learning disabilities or provide a truly integrated environment for activities that transcend cognitive ability.

Employment opportunities

Day services currently have only a limited ability to prepare people for paid employment or to assist in accessing employment opportunities (Beyer et al, 2004). More commonly, specialist supported employment services have developed, which not only seek to identify potential jobs but also to directly support people with learning disabilities as they enter employment.

> "What we say about supported employment is it's not about earning a wage, it's about achieving inclusion. Although people must have an equal wage to somebody else in the organisation – that is one of our strictest rules – but the real benefits are far beyond." (Commissioner)

Employment can offer people with learning disabilities a chance to genuinely become part of the mainstream and to begin to develop natural supports within the wider community rather than remaining dependent upon statutory services (Wistow and Schneider, 2003). Local authorities are well placed to lead the way as employers; as some commissioners were aware:

> "The council for a start could be an excellent employer of people with disabilities if it really got its act together." (Commissioner)

There was limited evidence that this was beginning to happen in a few local authorities in the study:

> "Our county council have been very good in not just producing a plan around supported employment, but actually making it part of their mainstream supported employment and mainstream public service agreement." (Commissioner)

It is in areas like this that networking, such as that enabled by Learning Disability Partnership Boards, can pay off:

> "I would hope that the local Partnership Board will help bring together the elements of industry and commerce and other organisations so that we're not just targeting Tesco's for a few little jobs, that we actually have a much better approach and help people access employment in a much bigger sector." (Commissioner)

However, despite being aware of the value of (supported) employment, commissioners still commonly perceived problems putting their plans and principles into practice. Part of the difficulty was that local services for adults with learning disabilities did not feel best placed to address the broader, national obstacles involved (see O'Bryan et al, 2000) such as the 'benefits trap':

> "If we can have a major change around benefit and other things like that, we'll get a lot more people into work. That's a big issue, it's a national issue and unfortunately I don't think that's picked up properly but there's not a lot I can do about that one." (Commissioner)

Even in areas where supported employment initiatives had been successful, there was a strong belief that employment should not be the responsibility of social care services:

five

"Social and health care commissions a number of providers to provide supported employment services for people with a learning disability. Our difficulty at the moment is that we've hit a bit of a block because we've got so many people supported in employment who still need support, and its finding the mechanism whereby we can continue to support those people but bring new people through. And we're tussling with that one at the moment and how best we manage that. We haven't found a solution yet – its money based – if I'd got more money I could do it.... I think that's where the link with the Department of Work and Pensions is key because I think they have a role here. I think we're, in terms of social and health care, actually doing too much – that it's somebody else's responsibility, but – as they haven't done it – we've really got to do something." (Commissioner)

As with housing, there was evidence from our research that commissioners were slowly beginning to develop partnership approaches to employment (see also the papers from the expert seminar organised on this issue as part of the research: Strategies for Change, *Appendix A*). The numbers of people with learning disabilities in work is low, but slowly increasing (Beyer, 2001). Effective partnership working with generic employment services and more active demonstrations of best employment practice by public sector employers will, it is hoped, result in a faster pace of change in the years to come.

Opening up community spaces

A more unusual option for the modernisation of day services pursued in some places turned the ordinary approaches to community integration on their head. Rather than taking people with learning disabilities out of day centres and 'into the community', day centres were being opened up for a wider range of community activities available to all members of the public, as this commissioner described:

"The approach we've had so far has been let a thousand flowers bloom, so we've been encouraging centre managers to follow up some of their good ideas locally. So I could point you to, for example, work that's going on where the local day service is becoming a community arts centre."

Such a method of encouraging social integration has yet to be tested and requires dedicated and resourceful staff if it is to work well. It is perhaps unlikely to be a desirable – or feasible – option for every day centre. But such an approach might enable some people with more complex impairments to continue to have access to buildings that are physically adapted to meet their particular requirements while not automatically restricting them to a wholly segregated social environment.

This chapter has intentionally avoided the fashion for illustrating points about practice with examples of individual successes. However, the following example was felt to be worthy of special mention. It demonstrates how a determined commissioner, by working effectively in partnership with other agencies, can help find solutions that meet even very complex needs. This story is particularly pertinent because it is also an example of how a person-centred approach enabled one young man with a learning disability to live in his home community, having previously been forced into an 'out of county' placement:

> "Housing, social services and education, we just didn't get on. I took on the services in 99 and within nine months we had our supported living strategy. We couldn't get housing to move and politically I had to get housing on board... they moved, we got the first person in a year after that, 2001, a young man who'd been in care.

> "I mean you look for litmus tests, this young man had been in care all his life, nowhere to put him, I asked the children's home to hold on to him until he was a bit older, he was 19 and they said 'No, he's 19 he's got to be out'. I said, 'Can you hold on 'till 20?' They ... there was an incident, four staff allegedly got assaulted. I was threatened with the health and safety executive. We had to put this young man into ★★★ it's the only place in the country. In

those days it was £2,700 a week; a complex case so we went 50/50 with health. And his behaviour got worse. And then the next you know, four months' time, they said 'An extra £400 please'.

> "So we got a three-bed council house, contract procurement. We haven't done this supported stuff living before and we haven't got the capacity. So to start off we wrote our own specifications, wrote our own tender. We used our own knowledge and we did it; we put this man back, put him in the house. And not only is it costing us £1,000 a week less, but he has his own tenancy, he has his own car and his challenges have all ceased because people work around his needs not around theirs.

> "And we now have 60 people in supported living." (Commissioner)

five

What happens next?

Commissioners and carers look to the future

It is a testament to the determination of people with learning disabilities, their families and to all those working to improve learning disability services that, more than three years after its launch, *Valuing People* is still regarded as a driver for change rather than having been relegated to gather dust on a shelf.

Commissioners in this study expressed confidence that they were beginning to develop services, in partnership, that could deliver on the *Valuing People* vision of rights, choice, independence and inclusion. One or two believed that they were already close to achieving such aims. Most, however, felt that realising these goals would require continuing long-term effort on the part of all stakeholders.

When asked to identify what they would most like to change about existing local services for people with learning disabilities, commissioners most often mentioned the need for cultural changes within organisations. Modernisation of day services came a close second, followed by a desire to expand job opportunities and improve options for young people at transition and, at a more fundamental level, to change attitudes towards people with learning disabilities in society at large.

By contrast, when carers were asked the same question, the most important issue for them was short break services – which were not mentioned as a priority by any commissioner. Carers, like commissioners, were also concerned to see cultural change within learning disability services and the modernisation of day provision. They also wanted better information about services to be made available; higher staffing levels; better staff training; and assessments of need that were both person-centred and took on board the views of family carers.

Although the priorities shared by commissioners and carers indicate that there is much common ground, the differences perhaps reveal a continuing failure to recognise and respond to the needs of family carers who, in the absence of integrated person-centred services, have continued to provide support for their loved ones. Both commissioners and carers appeared to be genuinely trying to ensure that the needs and wishes of people with learning disabilities were centre stage, but there was not yet consensus on the best means of achieving this.

Beyond 2006

The funding from central government, which has supported the implementation of *Valuing People* through the work of the *Valuing People* Support Team, comes to an end in March 2006. What will happen afterwards? It has been suggested by some commentators that, in political terms, what is needed is a 'policy addendum' detailing what parts of *Valuing People* worked, what parts did not work, and how the work started under the auspices of *Valuing People* should be carried forward.

As things currently stand, there remains a strong pool of goodwill 'in the field' towards the aims and aspirations of *Valuing People*. Recent months have seen the beginnings of significant changes to organisational culture within statutory services; for example, the number of people with learning disabilities who receive a direct payment has doubled from 750 to over 1,400 during 2003 (Greig, personal communication, 2004). However, despite some positive developments at local level, *Valuing People* continues *not* to be a priority for the government overall; in particular, it has little prominence within the NHS, where priorities are determined largely by those areas of work covered by a National Service Framework (NSF). (But, of course, people with learning disabilities should, in principle, benefit as much as anyone else from the NSFs on coronary heart care, diabetes, older people, and so on.)

Although the *Valuing People* agenda will continue to be important, the things that people with learning disabilities say matter most to them – housing, employment, relationships – are not necessarily within the power of local authority social services to deliver, at least not in a direct sense. So it is important that commissioners and other stakeholders focus on promoting change in generic services in addition to striving for improvements to specialist (segregated) social care services. In principle, Learning Disability Partnership Boards – where functioning well – should play a significant role in ensuring that the *Valuing People* agenda retains a high profile within generic services, such as housing, adult education, leisure and employment, that are key to enabling people with learning disabilities to enjoy varied and independent lives within their local communities.

The degree of progress made thus far by local areas could be measured against four broad indicators:

- Are local strategies in place?
- Are these being implemented?
- Is there evidence of subsequent change within services?
- Are key stakeholders (especially people with learning disabilities and their families) happy with the direction of change?

Rob Greig, Director of the Valuing People Support Team, has expressed a belief (Greig, personal communication, 2004) that those areas of the country that have so far made the most progress towards implementing *Valuing People* (in terms of these indicators) demonstrate the following characteristics:

- People with learning disabilities and their families are at the heart of decision making, at individual and organisational levels.
- Managers and organisations are open to change.
- Managers and organisations are 'outward-looking' and willing to glean ideas from other areas to enhance their practice.
- Specialist learning disability services do not 'hold on to' the change agenda but seek to actively involve generic services (for example, getting Connexions

involved in transition; getting housing department to write learning disability housing strategy).

It remains to be seen whether these positive beginnings can be turned into permanent change in the practice and culture of services provided to all people with learning disabilities everywhere.

Self-advocates' views on change

To end this report, and in keeping with the principles of *Valuing People*, the hopes and fears of self-advocates about 'change' expressed at a one-day workshop are presented. Participants had clear messages on 'change', both for other people with learning disabilities who were fighting to gain greater control over their own lives, and for senior managers in statutory and non-statutory services who might influence the direction of services and changes within them.

Wanting change to happen

The first message for other self-advocates was that they needed to prepare themselves for change by:

- wanting change in their lives;
- having dreams and thinking big!;
- talking to people that will listen;
- finding out about all the options; and
- being prepared to take risks – this needs good preparation and support, and also requires that the individual is willing to work hard to learn new skills.

Making individual changes happen

The second message was that certain factors can significantly improve an individual's chance of realising his or her goals for change:

- seeing other people make successful changes in their lives can prove that change *is* possible;
- getting support to speak up;
- talking to the right people – people who can help make change happen: this might include fellow members of an advocacy group, family and friends, care managers or other paid staff;
- having a plan – your own (person-centred) plan; and
- continuing to battle until change is achieved.

Campaigning together for change

There was also an awareness that sometimes change is hard for an individual to achieve alone. In these situations campaigning as a group may be the most effective way of achieving change. This kind of change is not about directly meeting individual needs, but can be used to pave the way for the introduction of more person-centred services, which in turn should enable greater choice, independence and control at an individual level. The messages here were that:

- It helps to share experiences: if you are having difficulties getting your voice heard within services, then it is likely that other people are too.
- Speaking up together can be more powerful than speaking up by yourself.

six

- Becoming part of a self-advocacy group can give people the confidence to speak up about the changes they want in their lives.
- Self-advocates can help represent the views of other people with learning difficulties who are less able to speak up for themselves.
- Through local Partnership Boards and the National Forum, self-advocacy groups can put pressure on local social services and on the government to make changes happen.

Messages for managers and commissioners

Finally, amidst all the positive talk about change, self-advocates also issued some words of warning for managers and commissioners of support services. They urged those people who, in a very real sense, still determine which changes will or will not take place in people's lives to remember the emotional impact that change has on individual lives:

- Change can be sad because of people or things we leave behind.
- Change can be hard if you leave a job or a place where you feel secure.
- Some changes may not be what we have chosen.
- Sometimes change is difficult because there is nothing else to do.
- Change can be good and bad (at the same time).
- Some changes take time to get used to.
- It is important to keep in touch with old friends when services change.

- Changes can take a long time to happen and it can be hard to keep being hopeful and battling.

This last is a message with which all those involved in the challenge of realising the aspirations of *Valuing People* – commissioners, managers, frontline staff, people in specialist agencies and those in generic services, families and carers and people with learning disabilities themselves – will surely agree. Change takes time, but as the evidence from this research indicates, it can happen – and it can make a positive difference to people's lives.

References

Aitchison, J. (2001) *Deciding together: Working with people with learning disabilities to plan services and support*, London: King's College, Institute for Applied Health and Social Policy.

Arblaster, L., Conway, J., Foremen, A. and Hawtin, M. (1998) *Achieving the impossible: Interagency collaboration to address the housing, health and social care needs of people able to live in ordinary housing*, Bristol/York: The Policy Press/ Joseph Rowntree Foundation.

Aspis, S. (2002) 'Self-advocacy: vested interests and misunderstandings', *British Journal of Learning Disabilities*, vol 30, no 1, pp 3-7.

Beart, S., Hawkins, D., Kroese, B., Smithson, P. and Tolosa, I. (2001) 'Barriers to accessing leisure opportunities for people with learning disabilities', *British Journal of Learning Disabilities*, vol 29, no 4, pp 133-8.

Beyer, S. (2001) 'Trends in supported employment', *Tizard Learning Disability Review*, vol 6, no 3, pp 30-6.

Beyer, S., Grove, B., Schneider, J., Simons, K., Williams, V., Heyman, A., Swift, P. and Krijnen-Kepm, E. (2004) *Working lives: The role of day centres in supporting people with learning disabilities into employment*, London: DWP.

Bliss, V., Emerson, E., Quinn, H. and Thomas, D. (1999) *NW audit of quality in residential supports*, Manchester: Hester Adrian Research Centre.

Bradshaw, J. (2001) 'Communication partnerships with people with profound and multiple learning disabilities', *Tizard Learning Disability Review*, vol 6, no 2, pp 6-15.

Brown, H. and Cambridge, H. (1995) 'Contracting for change: making contracts work for people with learning disabilities', in T. Philpot and L. Ward (eds) *Values and visions: Changing ideas in services for people with learning difficulties*, Oxford: Butterworth-Heinemann.

Cambridge, P. (1999) 'Building care management competence in services for people with learning disabilities', *British Journal of Social Work*, vol 29, pp 393-415.

Cambridge, P. and Brown, H. (1997) 'Making the market work for people with learning disabilities: an argument for principled contracting', *Critical Social Policy*, vol 17, no 2, pp 27-52.

Cameron, L. and Murphy, J. (2002) 'Enabling young people with a learning disability to make choices at a time of transition', *British Journal of Learning Disabilities*, vol 30, no 3, pp 105-12.

Cassell, C. and Symon, G. (1994) 'Qualitative research in work contexts', in C. Cassell and G. Symon (eds) *Qualitative methods in organizational research: A practical guide*, London: Sage Publications.

Cole, A., McIntosh, B. and Whittaker, A. (2000) *'We want our voices heard': Developing new lifestyles with disabled people*, Bristol/York: The Policy Press/Joseph Rowntree Foundation.

Cumella, S. (2003) 'Valuing assessments and reports? The impact of "Valuing People" on people with a learning disability', *Journal of Integrated Care*, vol 11, no 2, pp 3-8.

DETR (Department for the Environment, Transport and the Regions) (2001) *Supporting People: Policy into practice*, London: DETR.

DH (Department of Health) (1999) *Facing the facts: Services for people with learning disabilities: A policy impact study of social care and health services*, London: DH.

DH (2001a) *Building capacity and partnership in care: An agreement between the statutory and the independent sector social care, health care and housing sectors*, London: DH (www.dh.gov.uk/buildingcapacity/).

DH (2001b) *Valuing People: A new strategy for learning disability for the 21st century*, Cm 5086, London: The Stationery Office.

DH (2002a) *Keys to partnership: Working together to make a difference in people's lives*, London: DH (www.gov.uk/learningdisabilities/partnership.htm).

DH (2002b) *Towards person centred approaches*, London: DH (www.valuingpeople.gov.uk/pcp.htm).

Giraud-Saunders, A. and Greig, R. (2001) *Joint investment plans – A learning disability workbook*, London: DH.

Glaser, B. and Strauss, A. (1967) *The discovery of grounded theory: Strategies for qualitative research*, Chicago, IL: Aldine.

Greig, R. (2003) 'Changing the culture', *British Journal of Learning Disabilities*, vol 31, no 4, pp 150-2.

Griffiths, S. (2000) *Supporting people all the way. An overview of the supporting people programme*, York: Joseph Rowntree Foundation.

Harker, M. and King, N. (2003) 'Evaluation of the south west region housing strategies for valuing people', unpublished manuscript.

Harrison, R., Mann, G., Murphy, M., Taylor, A. and Thompson, N. (2003) *Partnership made painless: A joined-up guide to working together*, Lyme Regis: Russell House Publishing.

Heslop, P., Mallett, R., Simons, K. and Ward, L. (2002) *Bridging the divide at transition: What happens for young people with learning difficulties and their families?*, Kidderminster: British Institute of Learning Disabilities.

HSC 2001/016: LAC [2001] 23: *Valuing People: A new strategy for learning disability for the 21st century: Implementation*, London: DH.

Jacobsen, Y. (2002) *Making the jump: A guide to supporting adults with learning difficulties make the jump from education to employment*, Leicester: NIACE.

Knight, J. (2003) *Analysis of north west learning disability housing strategies* (www.doh.gov.uk/vpst/documents/NorthWestHousingReport.pdf).

Learning Disability Task Force (2003) *Making things happen: First annual report of the learning disability task force*, London: DH.

Lewis, J. and Glennerster, H. (1996) *Implementing the new community care*, Buckingham: Open University Press.

McGrother, C., Thorp, C., Taub, N. and Machado, O. (2001) 'Prevalence, disability and need in adults with severe learning disabilities', *Tizard Learning Disability Review*, vol 6, no 3, pp 4-13.

McIntosh, B. and Whittaker, A. (eds) (2000) *Unlocking the future: Developing new lifestyles with people who have complex disabilities*, London: King's Fund Publishing.

Marshall, C. and Rossman, G. (1995) *Designing qualitative research* (2nd edn), London: Sage Publications.

Maykut, P. and Morehouse, R. (1994) *Beginning qualitative research: A philosophic and practical guide*, London: The Falmer Press.

Mintzberg, H., Ahlstrand, B. and Lampel, J. (1998) *Strategy safari: The complete guide through the wilds of strategic management*, London: Prentice Hall.

Mir, G., Nocon, A. and Ahmad, W. with Jones, L. (2001) *Learning difficulties and ethnicity*, London: DH.

O'Brien, J. (1987) *A framework for accomplishment*, Decatur USC, GA: Responsive Systems Associates.

O'Brien, J. and Towell, D. (2003) *Person-centred planning in its strategic context*, London: Centre for Inclusive Futures/Responsive Systems Associates.

O'Brien, J. and Towell, D. (2004) *Building local capacity for person-centred approaches*, London: Centre for Inclusive Futures/Responsive Systems Associates.

O'Bryan, A., Simons, K., Beyer, S. and Grove, B. (2000) *A framework for supported employment*, York: York Publishing Services.

ODPM (Office of the Deputy Prime Minister) (2004) *Strategic partnering task force: Final report*, London: ODPM.

People First, Scotland (2003) 'From invitations to real involvement', *Tizard Learning Disability Review*, vol 8, pp 25-8.

Potter, J. and Wetherall, M. (1987) *Discourse and social psychology*, London: Sage Publications.

Ramcharan, P., Grant, G., Parry-Jones, B. and Robinson, C. (1999) 'The roles and tasks of care management in Wales – revisited', *Managing Community Care*, vol 7, no 3, pp 29-37.

Reynolds, F. (2002) 'An exploratory survey of opportunities and barriers to creative leisure activity for people with learning disabilities', *British Journal of Learning Disabilities*, vol 30, no 2, pp 63-7.

Robson, C. (1993) *Real world research: A resource for social scientists and practitioner researchers*, Oxford: Blackwell.

Rodgers, J., Townsley, R., Tarleton, B., Folkes, L., Mears, C., Levy, G., Waite, L., Managanda, S., Jones, J. and Thurman, S. (2004) *Information for all: Guidance* (www.easyinfo.org.uk).

Russell, O. (2001) 'Case registers, trends and commissioning', *Tizard Learning Disability Review*, vol 6, no 3, pp 14-17.

Sanderson, H., Jones, E. and Brown, K. (2002) 'Active support and person-centred planning: strange bedfellows or ideal partners?', *Tizard Learning Disability Review*, vol 7. no 1, pp 31-8.

Sanderson, H., Kennedy, J., Ritchie, P., Goodwin, G. (1997) *People, plans and possibilities: Exploring person centred planning*, Edinburgh: SHS.

Scott, J. (2003) *A fair day's pay: A guide to benefits, service user involvement and payments*, London: Mental Health Foundation.

Service Users Advisory Group (2001) *Nothing about us without us*, London: DH.

Simons, K. (1995) *My home, my life: Innovative approaches to housing and support for people with learning difficulties*, London: Values Into Action.

Simons, K. (1998a) *Home, work and inclusion: The social policy implications of supported living and employment for people with learning disabilities*, York: Joseph Rowntree Foundation.

Simons, K. (1998b) *Living support networks: An evaluation of the services provided by KeyRing*, Brighton: Pavilion Publishing.

Simons, K. (1999) *A place at the table? Involving people with learning difficulties in purchasing and commissioning services*, Kidderminster: British Institute of Learning Disabilities.

Simons, K. (2000) *Pushing open the door: The impact of housing options advisory service*, Bristol/York: The Policy Press/ Joseph Rowntree Foundation.

Simons, K. and Ward, L. (1997) *A foot in the door*, Manchester: The National Development Team.

Simons, K. and Watson, D. (1999) *New directions? Day services for people with learning disabilities in the 1990s*, Exeter: Centre for Evidence-based Social Services.

Sutcliffe, J. (1996) *Towards inclusion: Developing integrated education for adults with learning difficulties*, Leicester: NIACE.

Sutcliffe, J. and Jacobsen, Y. (1998) *All things being equal? A practical guide to widening participation for adults with learning difficulties in continuing education*, Leicester: NIACE.

Todd, S., Felce, D., Beyer, S., Shearn, J., Perry, J. and Kilsby, M. (2000) 'Strategic planning and progress under the All Wales Strategy', *Journal of Intellectual Disability Research*, vol 44, no 1, pp 31–44.

Townsley, R., Rodgers, J. and Folkes, L. (2003) 'Getting informed: researching the production of accessible information for people with learning disabilities', *Journal of Integrated Care*, vol 11, no 3, pp 39-43.

Valuing People Support Team (2003) *Valuing People – how are we doing? A self-help pack for Partnership Boards to check they are getting things done well* (www.valuingpeople.gov.uk/ partnership.htm).

Valuing People Support Team (2004) *Learning difficulties and ethnicity: A framework for action*, London: DH (www.valuingpeople.gov.uk/ documents/ EthnicityFrameworkMainText.pdf).

Ward, C. (2001) *Family matters: Counting families in*, London: DH.

Wistow, R. and Schneider, J. (2003) 'Users' views on supported employment and social inclusion: a qualitative study of 30 people in work', *British Journal of Learning Disabilities*, vol 31, no 4, pp 166-74.

Appendix A: Further sources of information

British Institute of Learning Disabilities (BILD)
A charitable organisation working towards better lives for people with learning disabilities. The site offers a large range of publications, including research reports, practice guidance and accessible information; also training and conference events.
www.bild.org.uk/

Choice Forum
See Foundation for People with Learning Disabilities.

Circles Network
Provides links to circles networks across the UK; information about how to set up a circle of support; and training on circles of support and person-centred planning.
www.circlesnetwork.org.uk/

Community Care
Website of the social care magazine; includes updates on all developments in social care and the option of weekly news e-mails.
www.communitycare.co.uk/

Community Living
Website of the quarterly journal dedicated to promoting the rights of people with learning disabilities.
www.communityliving.org.uk/

Easy Info
A website dedicated to making information easier for people with learning difficulties. Has a range of information and resources.
www.easyinfo.org.uk/

Federation of Local Supported Living Groups
This site contains details of local groups and of training events related to supported living. A quarterly newsletter and a variety of themed papers can also be downloaded.
www.supported-living.org/

Foundation for People with Learning Disabilities

This site provides news and information on learning disability issues. From here it is possible to sign up for free e-mail news bulletins and for the Choice Forum, a UK online information exchange on learning disabilities.
www.learningdisabilities.org.uk

Housing Options

This site provides resources for anyone concerned with the provision of housing for people with learning disabilities.
www.housingoptions.org.uk/

Independent Living Fund (ILF)

Information about the ILF which administers government funds to enable disabled people to receive care and support in their own homes.
www.ilf.org.uk/

Joseph Rowntree Foundation (JRF)

Independent social research findings on a wide variety of social issues, with particular emphasis on housing and social care, including disability.
www.jrf.org.uk/

King's Fund

An independent charitable foundation that undertakes research into health-related issues; available publications include a research-based series about innovative approaches to day services for people with learning disabilities.
www.kingsfund.org.uk/

Learning Disability Links

Provides links to many other UK sites that offer practice-based information about learning disability.
www.rnld.co.uk/

Mencap

This site provides information about Mencap campaigns, services and local groups. It also has accessible pages for use by people with learning disabilities themselves.
www.mencap.org.uk/

National Development Team

An independent development agency, offering consultation, training and publications, which aims to promote inclusion and ordinary lives for people with learning disabilities.
www.ndt.org.uk/

National Electronic Library for Learning Disabilities (NeLLD)
Part of the larger National Electronic Library for Health, this site provides access to current research in relation to the development and delivery of services for people with a learning disability.
www.minervation.com/ld/

National Forum for People with Learning Disabilities
This site provides information about the work of the National Forum. It also provides a database of links to local self-advocacy groups across England.
www.valuingpeople.org.uk/

National Institute of Adult Continuing Education (NIACE)
The leading non-governmental organisation for adult learning in England and Wales. Provides a range of information on advancing the interests of adult learners and potential learners, including adults with learning disabilities.
www.niace.org.uk/

Norah Fry Research Centre, University of Bristol
This site provides information about a wide range of research currently being undertaken into issues relevant to people with learning disabilities. It also includes the Strategies for Change web pages, which provide further outputs from this research project. Papers on housing, day services, employment, person-centred planning and quality assurance can be downloaded, as can accessible summaries of some aspects of the project.
www.bris.ac.uk/Depts/NorahFry/

Paradigm UK
The website of the Paradigm learning disability services consultancy and development agency; includes a downloadable newsletter and articles on recent policy as well as details of conferences and publications.
www.paradigm-uk.org/

Plain Facts
An illustrated easy-to-read magazine and tape for people with learning difficulties and their supporters, produced for the Joseph Rowntree Foundation at the Norah Fry Research Centre. The magazine is distributed free to self-advocacy groups across the UK and is also available on audiotape. Each issue focuses on the findings of a different research project.
www.plain-facts.org/

Strategies for Change
See Norah Fry Research Centre.

Survey of People with Learning Difficulties in England

This site gives information about a national survey of the lives, lifestyles and unmet needs of people with learning difficulties, which is being undertaken by a team of researchers from Lancaster University in collaboration with Central England People First. The final report from this work is due in summer 2005.
www.doh.gov.uk/public/ld-survey.htm

Supporting People

This is the site of the Office of the Deputy Prime Minister; it contains full details of all government guidance and reports relating to the implementation of the Supporting People programme of housing-related support.
www.spkweb.org.uk/

Values Into Action

Site of the UK-wide campaigning organisation that works to promote the rights of people with learning difficulties to become citizens with full access to the opportunities of ordinary community life, including information, news, events and publications.
www.viauk.org/

***Valuing People* Support Team**

Department of Health website, which contains downloadable versions of all government guidance related to *Valuing People*. It is regularly updated with new workbooks, reports and other materials designed to assist all those involved in the implementation of the White Paper, including a monthly newsletter.
www.valuingpeople.gov.uk/

If you do not have easy access to the Internet, or have difficulty finding out the contact details of any of the organisations above, you can telephone the Norah Fry Research Centre on 0117 923 8137 for further information.

Appendix B:
Research methods

The project was built around a number of distinct but interrelated strands, all of which had a bearing upon the core issue of strategic planning. Unless otherwise stated, all interviews were tape-recorded and transcribed in full prior to analysis of content.

1. A review of good practice in commissioning learning disability services

This took the form of a series of 'expert seminars' on some of the most important issues within learning disability services. Topics were selected to reflect the priorities of *Valuing People*, namely, person-centred planning, developing housing and support options, modernising day services, employment and quality assurance frameworks. Seminars took place at the start of the project, autumn 2001 to spring 2002, and helped to identify many of the key issues facing commissioners and providers of services. Papers from each seminar can be downloaded from the Strategies for Change project website (see *Appendix A*).

2. An analysis of the first round of Joint Investment Plans (JIPs)

JIPs were obtained from 104 English local authorities, from a possible total of 127, giving a working sample of 82% of all JIPs. In order to analyse the JIPs, a standardised tool was developed whose aim was to enable objective assessment of the extent to which each JIP had included the following:

- a statement of vision or values designed to underpin local service provision, which was in line with that of *Valuing People*;
- evidence that the JIP had been produced through agreement with key local stakeholders, including people with learning disabilities and carers;
- information about the local population with learning disabilities and its demographic profile in terms of age, ethnicity and support needs;
- documented patterns of current service provision, in particular information about people's housing situation and day activities, and about current public expenditure on these services;
- a 'gap analysis', indicating where more or different types of services were required, based on local knowledge of unmet need; and
- an 'action plan' aimed at tackling the problems identified in the gap analysis, including prioritised tasks, intended outcome measures and practical implementation details (that is, how *much* of *what* was going to be done by *whom* within what *time* scale and using which *resources*).

A standard assessment schedule was completed for each available JIP and the resulting data entered into an Access database. This allowed a quantitative analysis of the JIPs' content to be undertaken.

3. A user-led review of the involvement of self-advocates in Learning Disability Partnership Boards

A self-advocate researcher and a support worker from Swindon People First were paid to lead this strand of work.

Visits were made to eight self-advocacy groups across England. The groups were chosen largely on the grounds of geographical spread but selection was, intentionally, biased towards groups that were believed to be well-established. (As an indicator, all but one of the groups visited operated from their own offices.) This type of purposive (Robson, 1993), rather than random, sampling was used in order to maximise the chances of identifying examples of good practice, since well-established self-advocacy groups were believed likely to have had more success in getting their voices heard in the context of Partnership Boards.

During interviews, questions were asked about objective working practices in relation to Partnership Board meetings (for example, how often meetings were held; whether self-advocates were paid to attend) and the subjective experiences of self-advocates involved in the meetings (for example, whether their views were listened to with respect; whether they felt able to propose items for the agenda). During two of the research visits it emerged that members of the same self-advocacy group attended Partnership Boards in different authorities; this made

possible the collection of data on ten Partnership Boards in total.

An easy-to-read summary of the findings from this strand of the research can be downloaded from the projects website, see:

www.bris.ac.uk/Depts/NorahFry/Strategy/accessible.pdf

4. Interviews with carer members of Partnership Boards

A total of 17 interviews were undertaken with carer representatives on Partnership Boards. Three interviews were conducted face to face, the remainder by telephone. Carer representatives were approached by either commissioners or Partnership Board Chairs who had already been interviewed in the course of the project (see 5 below) or contacted us in response to a call for respondents posted on the Choice Forum website (see *Appendix A*). Topics covered during these interviews included how the interviewee had become a member of the local Partnership Board; whether any feedback was given after Board meetings to formal or informal groups of carers; practical arrangements for meetings; what decisions (if any) were taken by the Partnership Board; how carers were involved in planning prior to the formation of Partnership Boards; whether *Valuing People* was perceived as making a difference to local services for people with learning disabilities; and carers' wishes for the future.

5. Interviews with commissioners of services for people with learning disabilities and Chairs of Partnership Boards in 20 locations across England

Following analysis of the JIPs, a purposive

sample of 20 local authorities across England was selected for fieldwork (with an additional local authority selected for piloting the interview schedules to be used in the other 20 areas). Authorities were chosen for inclusion in this part of the study in order to include examples of a broad range of factors: geographical spread, including urban and rural locations; demographic indicators such as ethnicity and age profile of the local population; local authority structure – shire counties, unitary authorities, metropolitan boroughs; Best Value 'star rating' of the authority; the quality of its JIP; and places with known examples of good practice in a particular area, such as supported employment or person-centred planning.

In each location interviews were undertaken with the commissioner for learning disability services (or multiple commissioners where joint commissioning arrangements across social services and health had yet to be introduced) and the Chair of the Partnership Board. Interviews with commissioners focused on their experiences of implementing change and their progress towards the changes in both culture and practice that *Valuing People* demands. Interviews with Chairs focused more narrowly on the roles and work of Partnership Boards.

6. An evaluation of a development programme for commissioners of learning disability services

Paradigm UK and the National Development Team ran the commissioner development programme evaluated as part of this research. Courses took place in 2000 and again in 2001.

Two sets of telephone interviews were conducted. First the course faculty was interviewed in order to gather a clear picture of the course content. After this the course participants were contacted and interviews were conducted with 11 (out of a possible 18) individuals. Questions focused on the perceived benefits from attending the course; whether participants had tried putting new ideas into practice as a result of the course; and what outstanding needs they still had in relation to training and professional development.

These interviews were not taped; responses were coded during interview directly on to a standardised response sheet.

A note on the theoretical approaches underpinning the study and the analysis of interviews

In approaching a subject matter of such complexity, it was felt from the outset that a qualitative methodology, and hence a phenomenological rather than a positivist approach, would provide the most suitable philosophical underpinning (Maykut and Morehouse, 1994). It was hoped that this stance would enable the collection of 'rich' data with which to explore the relevant issues and would avoid limiting the potential scope of the research to the horizons prescribed by the *a priori* ideas of the researchers (Cassell and Symon, 1994).

The methodology adopted was informed by a number of different qualitative approaches, but design flexibility was given a higher priority than slavishly following any one system of data collection and analysis (Marshall and Rossman, 1995). Within this, the most significant influences were those of grounded theory (Glaser and Strauss, 1967) and discourse analysis (Potter and Wetherall, 1987). However, these texts were used to provide relevant theoretical and methodological insights rather than being adopted in full as research methodologies.

Grounded theory stresses the iterative process of research whereby researcher and participants create a shared understanding of the phenomena under examination. It was useful to this study because it promoted the concept that social research is best approached with an open mind and without a commitment to proving or disproving any one theory. Grounded theory espouses a belief that it is possible to approach a research topic without any *a priori* expectations. The idea that any research could be approached wholly without preconceptions was rejected for this project, since an interest in any particular field of enquiry must logically entail some small amount of knowledge of the subject and hence engender an outlook already shaped by this knowledge. Despite this caveat, the belief that the researcher should be as open-minded as possible remained central to the project, and the idea was embraced that theory should be generated from the data rather than imposed on it.

A broad appreciation of *discourse analysis* was also influential in the study, with its focus on words, as spoken in interviews or written in official documentation, and its assumption that the 'reality' of a policy or its implementation may vary according to the perceptions and understandings of the speaker. This approach helped in analysing interview transcripts, where contradiction and divergent views were commonplace, and in valuing the wide range of 'interpretive repertoires' that it afforded. It was also important in its emphasis on the idea of reality as a social construct that varies according to the individual experiences, whether professional, personal or socio-cultural, of each interviewee.